HAPPINESS IS A STATE OF MIND

HAPPINESS IS A STATE OF MIND

*How to create space for
happiness in your life*

His Holiness Gyalwang Drukpa
with Kate Adams

First published in Great Britain in 2014 by Yellow Kite
An imprint of Hodder & Stoughton
An Hachette UK company

1

A CIP catalogue record for this title is available from the British Library

Trade Paperback ISBN 978 1 444 78476 3
eBook ISBN 978 1 444 78475 6

Typeset by Palimpsest Book Production Ltd, Falkirk, Stirlingshire
Printed and bound by Clays Ltd, St Ives plc

Hodder & Stoughton policy is to use papers that are natural,
renewable and recyclable products and made from wood grown in
sustainable forests. The logging and manufacturing processes are expected
to conform to the environmental regulations of the country of origin.

Hodder & Stoughton Ltd
338 Euston Road
London NW1 3BH

www.hodder.co.uk

Here is a book of sensitivity, grace and wisdom. It cuts through the confusions that surround what it means to be truly happy. It shows us the obstacles that make us a stranger to ourselves, and a way of cultivating a spacious kindness towards these obstacles that allows them to dissolve naturally. It guides us through practices that can help us reconnect with life as it is rather than as we would wish it to be, and re-discover the deep peace, immeasurable and indestructible, that has been with us all along, hidden in plain sight. A wonderful book that will become a trusted friend and guide to all who read it.

Mark Williams
Emeritus Professor of Clinical Psychology
University of Oxford

Without appreciation, our life is like plastic. Not only do we have to remove the non-biodegradable rubbish from our external environment, we have to clear it from our minds too! This is the way that leads to sustainable happiness.

HIS HOLINESS THE GYALWANG DRUKPA

His Holiness the Gyalwang Drukpa is an active environmentalist, educator and the spiritual head of the Drukpa Lineage, one of the main Buddhist schools of the Himalayas founded by the great Indian saint Nāropā (1016–1100CE). 'Druk' means 'dragon' and also refers to the sound of thunder. In 1206 the first Gyalwang Drukpa, Naropa's reincarnation, saw nine dragons fly up into the sky from the ground at Namdruk and he named his lineage 'Drupka' or 'lineage of the dragons'. Bhutan, known as 'Druk Yul' or 'land of thunder dragons', honours the Drukpa lineage as its state religion. Popular in many countries, it is also the most prominent Buddhist lineage in India and in 2014 a commemorative stamp was issued by the Indian postal service to celebrate 999 years of the Drukpa lineage.

Compassion in Action

One of His Holiness's main focuses is on environmental preservation and education, which puts into action the core Buddhist principle that all beings are interconnected and interdependent. His mission is to promote universal harmony and inner peace by integrating the spiritual tenets of love and appreciation into daily life. His work also includes encouraging gender equality, establishing educational institutions, medical clinics and meditation centres and rebuilding heritage sites in the Himalayas. He is the founder and spiritual director of the award-winning Druk White Lotus School in Ladakh, India, which provides its students with a modern education while preserving their local culture.

Emphasising that everyone can have a positive impact on the community around them, His Holiness teaches that we should put compassion into action. In recognition of these activities, the Gyalwang Drukpa received the United Nations Development Goal Honour and Green Hero Award in 2010, presented by the President of India.

Gender Equality

Historically, women in the Himalayas have struggled to receive equal treatment, sometimes being ostracised for seeking to practise spirituality. The Gyalwang Drukpa is working to change this and has established the Druk Gawa Khilwa Nunnery – a modern and green abbey outside Kathmandu, Nepal with a satellite abbey in Ladakh, India. There, women receive a modern education, as well as spiritual training historically reserved for men. In an effort to instill self-confidence, the Gyalwang Drukpa has also authorised them to learn kung fu, training that was off-limits to women for over two centuries. These kung fu nuns are gaining worldwide recognition. A BBC News documentary featured them, in addition, they have performed at the Olympic Park in London and at the CERN in Geneva.

The Gyalwang Drukpa regularly addresses the international community on contemporary issues including environmental protection, gender equality and religious tolerance. Most recently, in September 2012, he attended United Nations week in New York, where he spoke at the United Nations Women's Forum, attended high-level meetings concerning the Middle East, and visited with United Women's forum including other notable presenters, such as Cherie Blair, Geena Davis and Her Royal Highness Princess Basmah bint Saud.

The Gyalwang Drukpa collaborates with well-respected international organisations to promote the message of active compassion. Most recently, the Gyalwang Drukpa visited the CERN in Switzerland to discuss the seeming tension of religion and science in society, as well as the improvement of gender equality. He recently visited the World Health Organization, to discuss, among other things, potential cooperation in improving health worldwide.

Live to Love

In his effort to use Buddhist approaches to solve modern day problems, the Gyalwang Drukpa founded the Live to Love global humanitarian movement in 2007. Live to Love is an international consortium of secular, non-profit organisations working together to achieve five aims: Education, Environmental Protection, Health Services, Relief Aid and Cultural Preservation.

Beyond its formal aims, Live to Love hopes to inspire others to integrate acts of love – big and small – into their daily lives.

Environmental Protection

The Himalayan region, known as the 'third pole' supplies water to nearly one-half of the world's population and is disproportionately impacted by global warming. Live to Love sponsors several unique and world-renowned projects focused on environmental protection of this fragile eco-system. For example, every year, Live to Love hosts the 'Eco Pad Yatra' ('Pad' means 'foot' and 'Yatra' means journeying, 'Pad Yatra' means 'journey on foot') a trek in which hundreds of volunteers hike hundreds of miles collecting plastic waste. Live to Love also plants literally tens of thousands of trees in the region, cleaning the air of toxins and stabilising the soil. In September 2013, during the UN week, the Gyalwang Drukpa was named 'The Guardian of the Himalayas' by Waterkeeper Alliance, founded in 1999 by environmental lawyer Robert F. Kennedy Jr. and several Waterkeeper organisations.

In 2010, the Gyalwang Drukpa launched an initiative to plant one million trees in Ladakh, as part of the 'one million trees' campaign initiated by Wangari Maathaï, recipient of the Nobel Peace Prize in 2004. As part of this initiative, the Gyalwang Drukpa led the Live to Love volunteers to break the Guinness World Record twice for most trees planted simultaneously. Most recently in October 2012, over 9,800 volunteers planted nearly 100,000 trees, safeguarding villages from mudslides and cleaning polluted air.

Education

The people of Ladakh, India, preserve a unique Buddhist lifestyle. As modernisation occurs, they are losing their indigenous culture and are having difficulty competing in the new economy. With approximately 1,000 students, the Druk White Lotus School (DWLS) seeks to provide its students with a modern education while instilling a respect for the unique indigenous culture of this region. This curriculum includes courses in English and computer skills, as well as the local language and art. DWLS has won multiple accolades for its sustainable design including three World Architecture Awards and the Inspiring Design Award from the British Council for School Environments. The school has been the subject of an acclaimed PBS documentary (USA), narrated by Brad Pitt, and has been featured in the Bollywood blockbuster film, '3 Idiots' starring Aamir Khan.

Medical Services

Many remote Himalayan communities lack basic medical services. The Druk White Lotus Clinic is located on Druk Amitabha Mountain outside of Kathmandu, Nepal, and provides regular medical care for the community living on the mountain and an annual 'eye camp'. Live to Love seeks to train amchis, practitioners of traditional Himalayan medicine, to provide basic medical care to very remote communities and liaise with allopathic doctors to treat more serious illnesses.

Relief Aid

Recently a flash flood from an unexpected cloudburst devastated Ladakh, killing hundreds and leaving thousands homeless. The Gyalwang Drukpa's Live to Love international and domestic volunteers distributed necessities to those in need. They provided nearly 300 units of LPG gas tanks and cooking stoves to displaced families to replace more dangerous portable kerosene stoves. The Druk White Lotus School took in children left homeless because of the flash flood. In light of this disaster, Live to Love seeks to train local Himalayan volunteers in disaster relief expertise in the coming years to provide a rapid, formal response to future events. The Gyalwang Drukpa himself visited, on foot, 50 remote villages affected by the flash flood.

Heritage Preservation

The culture and art of Ladakh, India is primarily Buddhist. Because Ladakh is located along the Silk Route, many locations present rare examples of Gandhara and Bamiyan style Buddhist art, which synthesises Byzantine, Roman-Greco, Scytho-Parthian and Indian elements. Most examples of this style of art have been destroyed in Afghanistan and Pakistan. At the instruction of the Gyalwang Drukpa, Live to Love seeks to preserve this unique art. In addition, Live to Love is beginning an initiative to digitally archive blockprints, manuscripts and texts found in community buildings and homes that reflect and chronicle the culture and history of Ladakh.

His Holiness the Gyalwang Drukpa sits on the Earth Awards Selection Committee along with Jane Goodall, Richard Branson and Diane Von Furstenberg. Spearheaded by Prince Charles of the United Kingdom, the Earth Awards Selection Committee identifies and recognises viable innovations that improve the quality of life.

His Holiness the Gyalwang Drukpa is an avid writer; he writes all the messages on his personal website.

www.drukpa.org

Contents

Happiness is not a possession to be prized, it is a quality of thought, a state of mind.

DAPHNE DU MAURIER, *REBECCA*

Introduction

There is no path to happiness.
Happiness is the path.
BUDDHA

Imagine a life free from comparison and feeling completely at ease. Imagine not wanting more.

Happiness isn't your right, it is your nature and your essence, it is at the very heart of your being. If you want to be happy, it won't cost you a penny because you already have everything in your hands to be happy right now. But you might be experiencing obstacles that are getting in the way between you and your happiness. You might not have realised that it has been there with you, all along.

There are many things in life that are beyond your control – you can't predict the future, you can't make a person love you, you will lose people that you love. But you can decide what kind of person you want to be, and you always have the freedom to think for yourself, even when it doesn't always feel that way. It is with your mind that you create your world, it is

1

your mind that is the creator of both your happiness and your suffering. Right now, it might feel as though your mind and your emotions are in control of you, rather than the other way around. Through a little training and practice, just as you can become fitter in body, you can soon become stronger and calmer in mind, allowing it to settle so that you're able to see your true nature, which is to say your happiness, shine from within.

Right now, you simply need to be willing to let go of the usual struggle and be willing to let things fall into the right place. It is time to act from your heart. It is time to stop worrying about all the things that you perceive are wrong with you or your life and appreciate what's right in your world. We all need to be reminded every now and again how precious our lives are and it's up to us what we make of it. As Buddha said many times, 'You have to tread the path for yourself. Everything is totally in your hands.' Believe and trust in yourself to allow a little more space in your life for happiness.

Part I

What is Happiness?

Life is not about waiting for the storm to pass; it's about learning how to dance in the rain.

VIVIAN GREENE

What does happiness mean to you? What does it look like? How does it feel? Is happiness eating an ice cream on a sunny day or holding hands with the one you love? Is it being very successful in your work and gaining the admiration of others or material things? Is it an experience – a fleeting, sensory moment; or do you feel like it is some kind of mirage – elusive, seemingly just out of your reach? Could happiness perhaps be something deeper, more meaningful, something that might infuse your whole life and way of being with joy and contentment? Might it create a foundation of strength, positivity and kindness from which you can go about your day and which you could bring to your choices, words and actions as you make your way along life's path? Could happiness be the reason things come together, rather than just the end result?

Life can seem very complicated, full of difficult choices and expectations, pressure to be this, that or the other. But at the heart of each day, for each and every one of us, there is the hope that we will be happy and free from pain, both here in this moment and within our lives as a whole. We want to be rid of the nagging feeling of 'not yet' happiness – that somehow if we can get all the conditions in our life just right, then we will be able to put our feet up and finally be happy. We want to feel good and relaxed in ourselves; we don't want to feel that underlying nervousness or sense that somehow, things aren't quite right. If we could just stop running around, we have a feeling that happiness might well find us, and yet we can't help but worry that if we stand still for a moment, we might not know what to do with ourselves.

Why do we seem to find so many obstacles in the way of happiness? And is happiness just a luxury anyway – something that it is selfish for us even to think about?

I don't think I have to convince you that happiness matters. I only have to ask you to look into your heart. And it's really quite a wonderful thing because one person's happiness has the potential to make another person happy, and the more people who are happy, the more chance we have to make the world a better place. Happiness affects all aspects of our lives: it gives us an advantage in our work, it helps us to be more healthy, it deepens our love for those close to us, it makes us more friendly to our environment, it makes us kind and caring people. These are all the extra bonuses that come with happiness; and happiness itself is a benefit of becoming closer to our inner nature, when we peel away all the layers of opinion, pride, self-criticism, expectations, hopes and fears that have built up over time. The tools offered later in the book all help to cultivate a happy state of mind and may be applied to all aspects of our lives, from being able to see situations from another point of view, to freeing the mind of comparison or complaint.

And the best news of all is that you are your own boss when it comes to happiness, however much you might think that other people pull the strings. It might take a bit of practice, but when you realise the true source of your happiness, then you can become great friends with it and share it with those around you. It can become a catalyst for great change, great love and great kindness.

1

Happiness is Your Nature

Nature never did betray
The heart that loved her.
WILLIAM WORDSWORTH

Creating happiness is not like following a cookery recipe. And when people say things like, 'Be positive', this is just placing another expectation or pressure on you.

But in fact, happiness is already there. And what you *can* get better at is realising that it is there – at nurturing and nourishing it with your mind and then your actions. Then, happiness blossoms. The mind's natural state is one of clarity and luminosity. And so if you engage in the process of developing it, you will be able to see as you have never seen before.

The true nature you were born with is quite beautiful and full of love. Happiness is your nature. You don't need to pursue it, and you don't need to worry that someone else might take it away from you. You just need to realise it is right there, in your heart, always. Sometimes it just gets hidden away or covered over, so you can't see it, but it's still there, whether the sun shines or the rain pours.

Some philosophers have described happiness as a fleeting moment, a sensation that can only come along once in a while (otherwise we wouldn't notice how much we like it). In a way this makes sense because we human beings are very talented at putting up obstacles between ourselves and our happiness – so much so that we only catch the odd glimpse of it beneath the turbulent surface of our minds that are filled with thoughts rushing around: worrying about life, worrying about what kind of person we are, what others think about us and why other people are so difficult all the time. But we can practise opening up our hearts and minds and allowing these glimpses to become wider and infuse our daily lives more.

Happiness is pleasure, of course. From eating a piece of chocolate to doing something we never thought possible – these are the fleeting moments of happiness. What we are really interested in, though, is developing a sustained sense of happiness from *within*. This happiness is our inspiration and motivation; it is our love, our empathy and compassion, our joyful effort and our generosity.

> *All that we are is the result of what we have thought: it is founded on our thoughts and made up of our thoughts. If a man speaks or acts with a good thought, happiness follows him like a shadow that never leaves him.* THE DHAMMAPADA

We often say that life is very rare and precious, so why do we let chances slip by? I advise my friends and students that they have to be smart, seizing every opportunity for self-improvement and not giving themselves excuses to turn them down. It is easy to fall into the habit of keeping so busy doing nonsense that you miss opportunities that are right in front of you. But I encourage you to grab them. I know it isn't always easy (sometimes I have to remind myself of my own advice), but as you cultivate and take care of your mind, it will take care of you and your happiness in this life.

Your sense of happiness right now, in this moment, is, of course, fed by your life experiences – how your day is going, how you feel about the person you are and the path you are walking. But why not take this opportunity to turn things around: see that it is your happiness that can feed your life, how your day is going and who you are. Nurture your mind to loosen its grip on worries or fear, pressures to succeed, resentments or regrets, and instead look with love and generosity, embracing the potential in uncertainty, letting others be themselves, finding your inspiration. Let go of the conditions that you might have been placing on your happiness up to this point in your life. You don't need a reason to be happy. Whether today is a challenging day, a creative day, a lazy day or a sad day, at its heart it can be a happy day.

THE BENEFITS OF HAPPINESS

Let's look at some of the benefits of happiness:
- We become more likable.
- We like people more.
- We are kinder, more compassionate and generous.
- We have more love in our lives.
- Our bodies are healthier.
- We have more clarity.
- We embrace our fears and uncertainties.
- We gain more fulfilment from our work.
- We learn and grow from our times of suffering.
- We learn not to take ourselves too seriously.
- We feel balanced and comfortable in our own skin.
- We flourish.
- We help others to flourish.
- *We help the world to flourish.*

Now let's look at each of these in a little more detail.

We become more likable

Smiling is contagious. Joy radiates. It's attractive to everyone else in the room. We can think a good thought about someone or we can talk to them with a smile in our hearts. When we are happy, we feel better about ourselves and, in turn, this means we find it easier to feel better about others, so that we may infuse our interactions with people with compassion. Kindness is a wonderful two-way street: like so many good things, the more we give it away the more it will grow in us, nourishing our happiness like water that we use to feed the flowers.

We like people more

It feels so much better to like people, rather than be agitated or upset by them. When you aren't feeling so good about yourself or your life it is easy to see those around you with the same negative perspective. But with a happy mind you see the good in people. One day, for example, you are tired and cranky and it's as though your partner can't do anything right, and then the next day you see the same person through completely different eyes. It is our own mind and our own happiness that determines how we see the world around us.

We are kinder, more compassionate and generous

It might worry us that happiness is something that is selfish and makes us too focused on ourselves as individuals, but people who choose happiness, especially the deep-seated contentment kind, will often do the most unselfish things of all. After all, when we are angry or upset how likely is it that we will give away our spare change to that man on the street? Happy people allow themselves to care deeply about others and their happiness, in turn; they have the strength to be able to walk a mile in another's shoes. When we create the space for happiness in our minds and our lives, we are able to see situations from all the different angles, rather than clinging to one rigid view of how the world or our lives should be. This gives us patience and tolerance for alternative points of view, so that we are less easily irritated or angered. We give people a break, rather than making our minds and our hearts small with things that don't matter.

We have more love in our lives

A sad effect of unhappiness is loneliness, which, in turn, feeds more unhappiness. There can even be a tendency to believe we are unlovable – or simply, that we will never find love. The trouble is that these kinds of beliefs then build barriers between ourselves and love. Our beliefs create our experiences and those experiences then reinforce our beliefs, generating a circle of unnecessary mental suffering. Conversely, a wonderful side effect of happiness is that as we give away kindness and compassion, so we will feel these things in return in our lives. Just as we allow ourselves to feel love towards others, we will keep down the barriers that might have prevented love from coming into our lives. For some people, it may be that they particularly need to focus on being kind to themselves, to believe that they deserve it, so that they will be able to receive it from others too.

Our bodies are healthier

Happiness is good for the heart; it is the best medicine for stress and it encourages us to look after our precious bodies a little more. It gives us a feeling of energy and vitality, so that our bodies may feel stronger and our minds calmer; whereas when the mind is unhappy, the body feels it too through tiredness or constantly feeling under the weather – that feeling of not wanting to get up in the morning. Even when the body falls sick, the happy mind is able to help alleviate the amount of suffering we feel.

In return, when we take care of our bodies, it gives a great support to the mind. At our nunnery, Druk Amitabha Mountain in Nepal, kung fu is taught and practised every morning. This isn't just aimed at physical fitness, but is also to give the nuns a boost to their confidence and self-esteem. Focusing on very specific movements of the body also seems to be a workout for the mind. It is the same with yoga – it is a meditation for the body. So if, for example, one day you are practising yoga and struggling very much with your balance, this will usually mean that your mind is a little off balance too!

We have more clarity

When the mind is happy it is like an ocean whose surface has become calm and the waves and sand that usually cloud the water have settled, so that we can see

13

right to the bottom. Just like the incredible coral reefs of our oceans, there is beauty we could not imagine and we have the chance to look at ourselves and our lives in this peaceful state of mind, so that we may get to know who we are and who we would like to be. There are no absolute rights or wrongs, but we are able to look into our hearts and find the aspiration and motivation to take action in our lives – to jump in.

We embrace our fears and uncertainties

When we are generally optimistic we no longer hold so much fear of uncertainty. We don't need to know exactly what will happen tomorrow or even today because we feel ok in ourselves, and with uncertainty may come exciting and spontaneous opportunities. Being comfortable with and accepting of uncertainty is one of the best ways that we can nurture happiness. When we have this flexibility in our minds we are far less likely to feel disappointed, either with others, with situations or with ourselves. We don't demand that things be a certain way in order for us to be happy – we go with the flow, easing our way around obstacles, rather than getting trapped by them.

We gain more fulfilment from our work

To be happy in our work is one of life's great gifts. We spend a great deal of time in activities we label as 'work' and we also tend to believe that with success at work will come happiness. But really, success comes from a happy state of mind, rather than the other way round. For me, one of the biggest aims of sharing the ideas in this book is to release the mind from all the conditions that we place on our happiness: that we will be happy *if this happens*, or *when we have achieved that*. When we are happy we are present in the moment, we are in the flow of our lives. And the same is true of our work: when we are lost in pure focus or concentration it is a great feeling. When we interact with others through our work and learn, teach, help or inspire we make great connections and enrich our minds and our lives.

We learn and grow from our times of suffering

Happiness sometimes gets a reputation for being unrealistic, for papering over cracks in our lives that are in truth very painful and difficult. This is why it is so important to acknowledge *all* of our emotions, positive and negative, and look them honestly in the face, rather than trying to ignore them. If we don't allow ourselves to understand our suffering, then the type of happiness we will experience will be superficial – like a plaster that covers up the cut, but doesn't heal the wound.

Many people might wonder what someone in my position would know about pain and suffering. How can a monk sitting on a mountain or in a cave have any understanding of what is happening in the real world? I appreciate every day that has gone by in my life, but I can't tell you that I was smiling with happiness all of those days. I was barely four years old when I went to live with the monks. I didn't see my parents for long periods at a time and I wasn't always very good at my studies; sometimes I was beaten – and I worried a great deal that I wasn't good enough to be the person everyone said I was. I have lost some of my beloved gurus along the way, and today I am at the top of the responsibility tree, accountable for hundreds of monasteries, nunneries and schools in the Himalayas. I say all this to show that it's not the case that I haven't had painful days or that I've never felt a burden in my mind. But all of these times of sadness or feeling out of my depth have been gifts to my happiness too. They have strengthened my appreciation of life, reminded me of my purpose and given energy to my work. They have been invaluable lessons in compassion.

We learn not to take ourselves too seriously

I sometimes think people may not take me very seriously as a monk as I am often to be heard laughing away like nobody's business. It is helpful to experience all of our emotions deeply, but it is also good occasionally to let go of being too serious, especially when it comes to ourselves. Being able to laugh at our own mistakes or mishaps means that we aren't tormented by embarrassment or worry about what others might think of us. It gives us the freedom to be that self that gives joy to others, rather than being caught up in our own fussiness or cynicism.

We feel balanced and comfortable in our own skin

With happiness comes contentment and peace. I know that in modern societies many people are taught that contentment isn't enough as they strive for success – if one goal or summit is reached, then they must find a bigger, higher one. And for some, it is the striving that is the enjoyable part, so that often they feel an anti-climax once they have achieved their goal, pausing only for a moment before looking around at where to go next. This is quite a stressful way of living – always looking for happiness around the next corner when it has been right there by our sides all along. It is possible to feel relaxed and friendly with our inner nature, to allow ourselves to feel happy, while also being very active and getting a good deal done. That way, instead of rushing from one experience or achievement to the next, we give ourselves the time to appreciate each moment of the day and embrace all of our emotions as they arise, without fear or judgment.

We flourish

To be happy is to thrive in one's life, rather than simply survive, and a happy state of mind can show the way towards a life that flourishes with a sense of meaning and purpose. What a gift we have in our ability to feel happiness. What a gift that so many of us don't have to worry about survival on a day-to-day basis and can therefore focus more of our efforts on making the world a better, happier place for all. When we give ourselves permission to be happy, we concentrate on the things we do well, rather than worrying about our imperfections. We release ourselves from the burden of constant comparison, guilt that we're somehow not quite good enough, attractive enough or successful enough. We free up so much of our mental time and strength. We aren't afraid or too shy to share our happiness, our love and compassion. We open up to the world's possibilities and beauty – and we flourish.

We help others to flourish

Here we are getting to the really big benefits of happiness. It is one thing for our happiness to help us flourish in our own lives, but then when we share happiness we go a step further and help other people's lives to be better too. It's a simple example, but think of the nurse who is happy in her life and her work – she shows true compassion to her patients and makes their day better, even when they are in pain. Her smile and her care can make all the difference, not just for the patients, but for their families too, even helping in the healing process. A little bit of shared happiness goes a long way.

We help the world to flourish

When we feel good in ourselves and in our lives, we *do good*. We become more loving not only to those closest to us, but we do our best to help make the world a better place, in whatever way we can – it doesn't matter how great or how small because it all counts. By doing whatever we can to take care of our minds and develop ourselves we, in turn, help to bring a little more peace to the world. I would even say that the greatest heroes of all are the peacemakers. So never be afraid that to uncover your own happiness is selfish, because it is *with* your happiness that you will take the best care of others, and you will appreciate this beautiful world that gives us all life and strive to take better care of Mother Nature too.

ARE YOU HAPPY TODAY?
ARE YOU HAPPY WITH YOUR LIFE?

Most folks are as happy as they make up their minds to be. ABRAHAM LINCOLN

To help us understand how your mind works, to see that the mind is the creator of everything, it is useful to consider what happiness and suffering mean to you, and how you feel about your life and your interactions with the world.

What do we mean when we say *happiness is a state of mind*? Can we really decide to be happy? Surely it depends on our circumstances, some of which will always be out of our control?

It's true that the external conditions of our lives are not within our control, but whatever our circumstances, we always have a choice as to how we decide to react to them, and about the person we make up our minds to be on any given day. It sounds simple. And we might well ask why human beings have had such trouble with happiness that so many books have been written through the ages. Why did the great philosophers all spend so much time thinking about it? But simple things aren't necessarily easy. Our minds are very complex and they are incredibly powerful; but in that power also lies the chance for misunderstanding and ego-building. So in order to help us choose to let ourselves be happy, there are many tools that help us to take care of our minds and allow our happiness to flourish. It is like the trunk and branch of a tree: if you look after the trunk very nicely by giving it water and keeping it at the right temperature, it will become very strong and well-rooted. Then, sooner or later, the branches will grow and will bear leaves, flowers and fruit without a problem. However, if you don't look after the trunk and the roots, these things will not grow.

Once we begin to take the time and effort to look at ourselves, those around us and our place in the world, we then begin to understand the simple equation of happiness: that it comes from within, that it grows with sharing, that it is our choice and that it provides the easiest route to becoming the person we want to be. It is then that we can stop wasting so much time worrying and instead be busy and creative doing good and positive deeds to help others. Our time and energy will expand, and we will remember every day what a precious life we have. It is a feeling of harmony, of knowing ourselves deeply and caring for others unconditionally.

Purity and simplicity are the two wings with which man soars above the earth. BUDDHA

Happiness is a balance both of our pleasures (which might change quite a bit from day to day, as our moods and emotions rise and fall) and our level of contentment (with which we evaluate how life is going and whether it is meaningful). It is possible to become caught up in associating happiness only with pleasure, while forgetting to nourish the deeper, underlying happiness, how we feel about life and who we are.

We spend *now* for the sake of happiness, but suffer at the end of the month. We break our diet today because we can't see clearly the true consequences of our actions. We confuse a sugar or alcohol high with happiness. We also seem to spend a great deal of time focusing on our unhappiness – our stresses and strains, the things we wish were otherwise. And that's why we look for the quick happiness fixes, the momentary pleasures that can give us temporary relief.

For lasting happiness we need to go deeper. But

this kind of deeper, contented happiness is often more elusive. It's not something we can create by eating a particular food or going to a movie. It is not easily defined and, in any case, its meaning might grow or change throughout our lives. We will never pin happiness down, we will never own it – and to try and do so would lead to destroying it in the long run. But we may come to know it better, and so be able to recognise it as a familiar friend, rather than a stranger. Happiness isn't something that we need to pursue relentlessly, chasing it all over the place, through the back streets that make up the map of our lives. All we need to do is to use our minds to shine a light on what is already there within our hearts, and to understand that we simply need to let ourselves be happy.

This is a cool, fresh feeling. It is when we feel a sense of space, and rather than grabbing for the next piece of entertainment or distraction for our minds, we instead enjoy and embrace the gap. We don't fill it up with unnecessary nonsense, but let it be – because it is our nature. By using the tool of awareness we not only find it a little easier to let the space develop between our thoughts, but also acknowledge feelings of agitation when they first begin to appear, and so deal with them quickly rather than constantly pushing them down or running away from them until they become like wounds in our minds.

It's important to go through all of these things and to truly experience life, and then build your awareness so that you begin to see and feel the difference between the burning types of happiness and those moments of a deep, connected sense of happiness. This is a deep love, a deep understanding; it is something immeasurable and also indestructible. Your inner happiness is *always* there – it's up to you to uncover it. It is something you can feel very safe with, even if you don't feel it directly all the time, and you can rely on yourself and your happiness as you go about your daily life.

2

The Obstacles to Happiness

If there are so many benefits to being happy, why do we struggle with happiness? What are the obstacles that come between us and our happiness, that stop us from being our true, authentic, kind, generous and fulfilled selves? Where do they come from?

We cannot control the things that happen to us or outside of us: if we do not have enough money to keep a roof over our heads or food on the table, then our happiness will be affected; other people may harm or try to harm us, or we may become ill or injured in an accident and experience great pain.

There is a great deal, however, that is in our own hands when it comes to happiness and living the life that we know we want to when we listen to our hearts. The life we have is so precious, and each of us has so many things to contribute. So why do we bury ourselves under the mental weight of expectations, worries and misunderstandings, creating disharmony within ourselves and with others, making ourselves unhappy in the long run? How do these 'happiness obstacles' build up over time? Why are we so often our own worst enemy?

It is the barriers we create in our minds that get in between ourselves and our happiness; they are like invisible walls constructed from our fears, our impatience, jealousies, anger and all the opinions and ideas that we cling to for our sense of identity. We want and expect things to be a certain way – so much so that sometimes we ruin our chances for happiness before we have even begun. Or we fit our minds into a mould of what we think is 'right', becoming too solid, too inflexible. We weigh down our happiness and close up our minds, rather than letting them float and wander around freely, so that they might open up to many inspiring new ideas and ways of seeing.

THE ROOTS OF OUR SUFFERING

It isn't what you have or who you are or where you are or what you are doing that makes you happy or unhappy. It is what you think about it. DALE CARNEGIE

Before we can truly begin to cultivate a happy state of mind, we need to understand the source of our suffering, the obstacles that come up between us and our happiness. It may be surprising, but when we begin to think through the things that we believe take away our happiness, it is possible to see how all suffering stems from the mind.

Of course, with physical pain, there is a sensation in the body which can be very intense. There is no questioning that pain feels very real. However, even with physical pain the level of suffering we experience comes from within our minds – how we cope with it, how we react to it on an emotional level.

Likewise, when we lose a loved one, grief and sadness will become our companions for a time while we heal from the pain of the loss. But it is through this type of suffering that we are able to truly understand our joy and happiness too. We are reminded of the preciousness of life, how important it is to live for each day, to embrace the present, rather than living in the past or constantly being anxious about the future. Our grief shows us how much we love and how much we care; it is then up to us whether we hold on to that grief for too long, undermining our

26

happiness and keeping us trapped in a very dark place or whether we have the courage to let our grief and sadness go.

Conditional happiness

So many people believe that if only they can achieve a particular goal – losing a certain amount of weight, perhaps, or getting top marks in an exam – they will be happy. Or they might think that if they can endure their job for now, it will bring them happiness through the money they can spend in retirement or through the security of knowing they can repay their mortgage. People are taught this way of thinking – of putting off happiness or imposing certain conditions upon it. But when we place conditions on happiness we are really limiting ourselves. What if we don't lose that weight or we don't get top marks? Does it really make a difference to who we are and should these conditions stop us being happy? We don't *deserve* to be happy – happiness is our nature, it is part of us, not an exchange. So don't put your happiness in a box marked 'only for special occasions'.

Expectations

When I teach, I talk a great deal about expectations, and how they have become an epidemic that is putting off happiness for people all over the world. Expectations are considered by many to be a very good thing

– they help people to strive for success, to make a good living for themselves and their families and to reach great heights. From my point of view, however, expectations are related to being overly outcome-driven, so again, it is a matter of creating a list of conditions or goals that have to be met before we can really say we have 'made it' and allow ourselves to be happy; and when we don't reach all our goals we feel disappointed.

If you can practise being intention-driven, then you do not rely on one particular outcome, so long as you have tried your best. When you place too much emphasis on outcomes, you are too attached to an imagined future. If you focus on your intentions, you become more present – what matters is what you are doing right now. Your intentions are based on your values, they are connected with your heart. This isn't to say that you abandon all goals, for example goals like gaining an educational degree or a promotion at work can be very helpful in encouraging ourselves to grow and fulfil our potential, but that you put the emphasis on your intention, why you want to do these things, rather than being attached to specific outcomes. The irony is that the more you concentrate on your intentions and values, the more effective you become at fulfilling your goals, too, because what you do during the day becomes aligned with your purpose. Happiness becomes the journey, not the destination.

Here is an example. In the morning you may set your goals for the day, such as spending more time with your family or getting through your 'to do' list at work. And then at the end of the day you become disappointed as you realise there are still so many things you wanted to do but weren't able to. If you focus on your intentions, instead, you may begin the day with a simple desire to express your appreciation for the people close to you and to make the most of the day. You focus on what you do, rather than worrying about what you haven't done. A moment spent with your loved ones might be fleeting but counts for so much because you are right there, happy in their presence. It's a change in your perspective.

You can also be a much more flexible person in this way, open to all the possibilities of an uncertain future. Expectations come with the potential for much disappointment, whereas intentions simply get you into a good frame of mind, from which anything might happen and you no longer need to feel attached to one specific outcome. Life rarely goes according to plan, so why make a trap for your own happiness by placing the burden of expectation on it?

When we lose our way

One of the biggest obstacles to happiness is when there is a disconnect between what we know in our hearts is the right thing for us to do and what we actually do. It is not always easy to match up our purpose with how we think, speak and act, but the more we can do this, the more productive and connected we will be.

Many people feel that they would be much happier if they could strike the right balance between work and life. Sometimes I think we forget that work *is* life, rather than being something separate that we put up with so that we can have a comfortable life the rest of the time. How people feel at work becomes a barometer for happiness, a rollercoaster of good and bad days with so many potential saboteurs, from bosses to feeling the weight of responsibility, to things going wrong or feeling overwhelmed and exhausted.

If you ever feel that you have somehow lost your way, or you are not sure which direction to take, meditation and mindfulness can help you to see beneath the choppy surface to the clarity within (see pages 41–60). Have the courage to keep going and bring your attention right into the present moment to look around you and see what is really going on in your life. Resolve to sweep away your doubts and uncertainties and grab today for all it's worth.

Habits of the mind

Our mental habits have a way of getting in between us and our happiness, especially if we are unaware of their strength. Over time we develop patterns in how we react to situations or people – we feel crushed by criticism, angered by people who bump into us, for example. We might wish we could react differently, but our habits are so entrenched that we fall back on them without thinking. We seem to follow the same negative patterns of thinking and behaving over and over again, and we're not sure how to break the cycle.

By bringing our attention to the present moment we can see those habits and patterns as they happen and understand what triggers them; by developing self-awareness we can choose not to follow the same old ways of thinking and strike out on a new path.

Negative emotions

Anger and its relations – such as frustration, impatience, intolerance, shame and guilt – are very corrosive to our state of mind. They cause us pain in the moment because they literally burn us, and when we react very suddenly or without thinking, we may lash out with words that act like arrows directed at other people, objects or situations. Unnecessary mental sufferings such as doubt, desire and greed take up so much precious space in the mind and can even make us small-minded. They also cause distance and separation; we want to get away from a person or situation we don't like, or from ourselves. We may even take something that is happening in the moment and project it as a universal truth that is never going to change: *I'm always going to be alone*; *I will never be happy like this.*

When we are angry, we can't see straight and we make rash interpretations and associations. If we are not careful of the anger that rises in the moment, it can become a more general anger towards life.

Similarly, the other emotions related to it can become habitual, so that we may tend towards comparison and jealousy or being suspicious of the intentions of others. This leaves very little room for joy and happiness in our thoughts and our hearts.

This is why it is so important to become more aware of and friendly with all our emotions; to explore the source of any negative emotions or feelings and to practise their antidotes – patience, appreciation and acceptance. An angry or jealous mind can never be happy, so for the sake of ourselves and those around us we need to understand our emotions and learn how to let them go.

Ego-clinging

In our teachings we talk a great deal about 'grasping attachments' and impermanence. The ego is a collection of all the stories and beliefs we have been told and have told ourselves about who we are over the course of our lives. When we become too attached to this identity, we limit ourselves and, as a consequence, we put limitations and conditions on our perception of happiness. And just as we cling to our egos, our egos cling to possessions and opinions in an attempt to feel secure. This creates an underlying sense of fear – fear that we might turn out to be 'wrong', fear that we might become losers in some way, fear of what others think of us.

If you are unhappy with yourself, then that is

because you haven't got to know your true self. You only know your ego, which right now is doing you a disservice and trapping you in unhappiness. The things that you do not like in your personality or about your actions are not *you*; and although it might seem impossible when you are consumed by feeling bad about yourself, you can begin to gently break free from the bonds of these labels. By taking care of your mind, you can transform your thoughts and your actions. In other words, you can transform your life.

Relationships

If you feel you are unhappy because of how people are treating you, the first thing to realise is that whatever others may say or do, you still have some degree of control over your reactions. If your happiness is within, then you don't have to let external conditions have such a hold over it. Sometimes our perception of intention – behind harmful words especially – is entirely different from or an exaggeration of what someone else was thinking.

There may be times when it does seem as though someone truly wants to upset or harm you with their words or actions. It is very hard for this not to affect your sense of happiness, but it may help to understand that their motivation for engaging in harmful words or deeds says everything about them and nothing about you. Although directed at you like a poisoned arrow, they have nothing to do with who you are, stemming rather from the person's own misunderstandings about who they are.

Contemplating and understanding this may help to reduce your sense of suffering and to see that other people don't need to become a fixed obstacle to your happiness. You may focus instead on all the positive relationships and connections in your life and nourish them with your happiness.

Fear and uncertainty

We feel our fears and anxieties in our bodies; they are obstacles to happiness that sit in the pit of our stomachs or make our whole being feel agitated and uncomfortable. Fear in itself is not the problem here though; our fears are some of the best signposts towards growth, towards doing what we really want to do and being who we want to be.

It is when you let fear and uncertainty about what may (or may not) happen fester, rather than facing them, that they can get in the way, between you and your happiness. Your ego will cling on to fear, but your true nature is fearless and free. You just have to peel back the layers, look directly into your heart and see the courage and confidence that lie within.

If you feel unhappy because of the situation you find yourself in, you can begin to explore the feelings it brings up for you and see if you can look at them – and the situation itself – from different angles, rather than believing them to be only a source of unhappiness.

When it comes down to it, no matter how many self-beliefs, circumstances or people we feel are lessening our happiness, we do have a choice when it comes to how we cope or deal with them in our minds. Do we hang on to frustration experienced during a morning meeting all day, so that we end up taking it home with us? Do we always take on the blame or responsibility for situations when they could easily be shared? Do we even worry a little about letting ourselves be happy, fearful that we might hurt so much more if it is then taken away from us?

We human beings seem to find complication and even suffering to a degree easier to deal with than happiness: it is easier to complain than to celebrate; it is easier to list what we didn't get done today, than to acknowledge everything we accomplished. We wrap ourselves up in expectations and ideas about how we think things should be; and we worry that contentment and peace will bring laziness.

I believe it is time you freed your mind and let happiness back in – it's been waiting patiently for you to open the door for long enough. The happier you allow yourself to be today the happier you'll be tomorrow and for the rest of your life.

3

A Happy Heart

Some pursue happiness – others create it.

RALPH WALDO EMERSON

If we can begin to understand the mind intellectually at first, then we will have made a good start. If we can begin to discover the sources of our happiness and also the sources of suffering, then we have a chance. But that isn't quite enough, as this kind of intellectual knowledge has to be brought down to the heart. When you are making a decision like buying a house, for example, you have all the facts and figures before you, but what really clinches it is the feeling in your heart: that's what you need to practise more, every day.

You probably know people who seem to know themselves – who are able to listen to their own nature. They experience just as much sadness and anger and desire as the next person, but are good navigators through even troubled waters. I have many friends who aren't religious at all, but who are simply in touch with themselves, which makes them very enjoyable and inspiring to be around. Even if they are on a path to some form of improvement, which may take quite some time, they are making the most of their journey, wherever it might twist and turn.

If we do not immediately identify with that sort of natural happiness, we can develop it. We can improve on our understanding of our own nature and we can reveal our happiness. This is my own experience.

What if we were able to simply choose happiness? What if we decided to do away with all the conditions, comparisons and expectations and focused instead on all the opportunities and truly good things we have in our life right now, today? People worry that if they are optimistic or look on the bright side they will set themselves up for a fall or a disappointment. But an optimistic mind doesn't expect every day to be a breeze or go perfectly according to plan; an optimistic mind has the flexibility to accept whatever does come their way and try to see the potential good in any situation. An optimistic, or *happy* mind embraces the uncertainty of life and is less attached both to material things and the way things are.

So, if this is the case, can we therefore train our minds to be happier, both in the moment and about who we are and what we've done, how we evaluate our life? The good news is that we can.

We need to reconnect with our true selves, our intuitive selves. This practice plants the seed of understanding, and with understanding, happiness not only becomes our state of mind, but we begin to share it with others all day long – through our thoughts, words and acts.

Both meditation and developing your general sense of awareness are very helpful for turning up the volume on your inner voice so that you may know your purpose and then align what you do on the surface of life with what is in your heart. You can then begin to look at the situations in your life differently. You will gain a fresh take on old patterns that have so often repeated themselves, and on things or people who you have always thought have somehow prevented you from being happy. You can also view challenges that arise more suddenly with a different way of seeing, so that you are less likely to be thrown off balance by things that usually sabotage your general state of happiness. You can pause . . . before you react.

With a little practice, you will begin to see the fabrications you have allowed to build up over time, the conditions and demands you have placed on life so that you might 'be happy'. You might discover that you have become very attached – even addicted – to certain ways of thinking, likes and dislikes; and you might have become narrow and closed off. It's not so easy for a narrow mind to be happy, so you need to practise opening your mind up, so you might let more happiness in.

Don't be afraid to ask yourself some direct questions:

- What is happening in your life?
- Do you *feel* happy?
- What is already good in your life?
- What do you really want to improve?

This is not to put pressure on you, but to help you realise just how much of the way you feel about life and experience comes from within your mind, and how spending a little time taking care of it may bring you great benefits.

If you are someone who tends towards more negative thoughts or emotions but know you would like to feel lighter and happier in yourself, you might be a little afraid of spending time with your mind, of looking directly at your emotions. But it's very important to know that even very negative emotions, such as jealousy, are never permanent – they come and go and are valuable for your life's journey.

There is no essential need to become attached to negative emotions, yet some people find it an easy trap to fall into. Others find the lure of optimism or a 'nothing-gets-to-me' attitude very strong and will ignore the presence of anything potentially negative; everything is like water off a duck's back to them, not even scratching the surface. But if we walk the middle way, we will maintain our balance: we will not be too upset by negative emotions or experiences, but equally we won't find that our egos are floating all over the place, knocking things over.

We need to be able to look at ourselves in the

mirror without squirming and be honest about the things we would like to improve and practise. When we are both kind and honest with ourselves then we can be kind and honest with everyone else, which brings so much peace and happiness into our minds and our lives. We begin to have a great capacity for empathy and compassion because if we are more sensitive and aware of our own source of happiness and our own vulnerabilities and quirks, then we will be more sensitive to the needs of others and how we may contribute to their happiness. We will be less quick to get caught up in criticism and judgments and will learn to live and let live a little more, while also striving to be and do the best we can in our own lives.

Have the courage to put your hand up and say it's time to face what is getting in between you and your happiness – then you give yourself the opportunity of your lifetime.

4

Getting in the Happiness Frame of Mind: A Practical Introduction to Meditation and Mindfulness

When you run after your thoughts, you are like a dog chasing a stick: every time a stick is thrown, you run after it. Instead, be like a lion who, rather than chasing after the stick, turns to face the thrower. One only throws a stick at a lion once.

MILAREPA

In combination with everyday mindfulness, meditations are excellent tools that give our minds a chance to nurture happiness. I have been trained to meditate throughout my life and so it comes as second nature, but I know that most of my friends find it quite difficult to sit still even for five minutes.

Let's think about how this modern way of living might be affecting our minds: many of us are constantly running after our wild, untamed thoughts, and because we have no control over them, our words and actions can be out of control too. So we react to situations in a split second, not giving ourselves a chance to make sense of things or to give ourselves a little bit of space. We have lost the pause button.

The first benefit of meditation is that it may help to create a sense of calm and, for a few minutes at least, some peace of mind. Meditation begins to makes our thoughts more friendly: they start to listen to us, rather us being controlled by them. So we are free to tell them, 'Ok, you guys, don't disturb me for five minutes.' This type of calm-abiding meditation is a good tool for slowing things down in the mind for a little while – for giving it a well-deserved rest.

WHY MEDITATE?

If we think of meditation only as calming the mind, as soon as we carry on with our day the same mental habits will come back and upset the balance all over again. I am therefore going to introduce you to all the other reasons why we practise meditation and awareness, so that rather than just calming the mind, you can begin to *transform* it, changing your life for the better.

• Meditation gives you the opportunity to deepen your appreciation of life. Appreciation is always there, underneath all the mental chatter, buried beneath our hopes and fears, but with meditation it is lifted up for a few minutes, so that we can really feel and experience it.

• When we use meditation to explore our feelings or to acknowledge past hurts, so that we may begin to let them go, deep-seated and difficult emotions may rise to the surface – emotions that we have been suppressing over time. This takes courage, but when we look directly at such thoughts or emotions in the safe space of meditation, we begin to see that it is up to us whether we continue to let them shape our reality and cloud our lives. What meditation always does is open up a sense of spaciousness in our minds, so that we may either take a mental break or have the chance to contemplate life honestly. We cling less to our thoughts or emotions and allow them to flow more freely.

• Meditation, and also developing an awareness of

ourselves and the world around us, encourages us to stop chasing after happiness and enjoy its presence in our lives today. We can be happy now, rather than rushing through the day, trying to tick things off on an endless to-do list, so that only then can we let ourselves be happy – when we have done enough to deserve it or to earn it.

- Meditation opens up our minds and allows us to see things differently, to explore the meaning of our lives and develop ourselves. We free our minds from the everyday constraints of worries or doubts and create space, so that we can ask ourselves how our happiness is doing today.
- Meditation allows us to understand the nature of time and how nothing is permanent in this life; through this kind of contemplation we are able to feel less clinging towards our expectations of what life needs to be in order for us to be happy. Through contemplating and reflection we begin to understand how our minds work, how all of our thoughts are perceptions – just one way of seeing – that might be perfectly valid, but that another view is equally valid too.
- We might contemplate the relationships we have with our loved ones, our friends, colleagues and with strangers that we encounter on the street. Are we treating others as we would like to be treated ourselves? If someone has upset us, can we look at ourselves in the mirror and think about how to improve, rather than be so quick to judge or criticise others?
- We might also contemplate our relationship with things

– with our possessions and with money, for example. Do we allow these things to flow in our lives, or do we grasp for them a little too tightly? It is when we begin to cling to anything or anyone that we make our minds inflexible and we begin to cover up our natural state of happiness with expectations and conditions.

You have to sit to see your mind

Nicole came to a retreat at Druk Amitabha Mountain in Nepal and shared her experiences of meditation:

I find meditation very helpful in combination with learning about, reflecting and contemplating aspects of the teaching or philosophy – the Dharma, as we say – which is really contemplating life. When I first began meditation I could only sit for a short time – five minutes, perhaps, if I was lucky. I still don't have a blank mind when I meditate, far from it, but over time the space between my thoughts has become wider. It's a case of watching your thoughts, observing them, but not holding on to them; so you let them go, drifting off the canvas of your mind. Sometimes they will be related to a teaching, like patience, for example, and it will be interesting to see what thoughts come; but equally, I allow them to move on, like a movie screen.

After doing this many times, your rushing thoughts will begin to slow down, so that you may see them more clearly and begin to detect a little bit of space in between. That is the space which allows our authentic

happiness to come from within and show itself to us.
This is a very nice state of mind to be in.

Putting things into perspective

Contemplative meditation helps us out of negative thinking. It offers a place to pause, and a chance to reflect. When we are stuck with negative thoughts we dwell on our own bad luck: why me, we ask. But when we give ourselves a chance to quietly contemplate things like our anger, jealousy or fears we can investigate without feeling so trapped. We can genuinely ask why we are feeling such emotions and look within for the answers, rather than finding reasons that are beyond our control.

It is easy to go through our days at such a pace that we miss such chances to contemplate and develop our understanding of life and who we are. We are too excited or too anxious to stop and think. When we are upset, especially, we don't have the energy to investigate, or maybe the self-esteem.

The mind is the base – it is the source of most of our suffering and our happiness. In Buddhism the mind is more to us than just intellect; we consider it to include the heart also, our 'nature'. Each of us is connected through the heart to the entire universe, and so if you get into the mind, you will see the universe.

YOGA FOR THE MIND

We have a practice that is called Guru Yoga. It is a series of meditations that we do which are, in some ways, like yoga for the mind. Just as physical yoga trains the body to be strong, yet flexible, the same goes for Guru Yoga and the mind. Often, we allow our emotions, stresses and strains to tense our shoulders up (this can be seen in the way people sit and walk hunched over), so most people's centre of gravity nowadays is in the shoulders. Yoga and sitting for meditation encourage the body's centre of gravity to sit below the navel, where it can offer the greatest stability.

When you first take up meditation or yoga, you might find it is very painful to sit straight for long periods of time, that you want to fidget and move around and that it's unbearable to sit still. It's the same for the mind. It can feel very uncomfortable at first to let our minds settle; we would almost rather they keep whizzing and whirring, filled with distractions from the main questions of our lives. We have to make a big effort to sit quietly and bring ourselves back to our centre.

It is fascinating to me how these old practices offer a sequence of mental exercises or meditations that are just as relevant to life today as they ever were. For example, at the beginning we simply generate our motivation: we remind ourselves of our purpose in life, which is basically to help as many people and

47

living beings as we are able to. This is all well and good for us monks and nuns, but what is the relevance for people living in the real world, you might ask. When you think about it though, can't the purpose of every single person be to do their best to make the world a better place in whatever way they can? To bring happiness and security to their loved ones? To spread tolerance and compassion?

We use meditation to visualise the wisdom within us all, our true nature. Other meditations include simply contemplating how precious life and our mental freedom is, which might help to release us from our usual limiting mental bonds such as expectation or falling into the trap of often complaining about what we don't have or what went wrong today rather than all the amazing things we already have in our lives and the things that went well today. What a great fortune life itself is.

We also use meditation to contemplate the nature of change and its inevitability. It is amazing how much mental unhappiness seems to be related to people either fearing change or trying to make or keep things just so.

It is really a very good way to help us to find our motivation, set our intention and take just the smallest steps towards developing our awareness of our inner wisdom, which is to say our inner happiness. It also creates a beginning awareness of how we use our thoughts, words and actions throughout the day. Often, we don't even realise that our bodies, speech and minds are connected and that the quality of our thoughts leads to the quality of our words and actions. And so simply by setting our intention at the start of each day we will begin to change the usual unconscious patterns – or, if we don't change them to start with, we will at least begin to notice them. This is itself a very good step and takes quite a bit of practice. We will only be able to let go of the obstacles between us and our happiness if we are willing first to recognise them.

Meditation is a way to calm things down so that you are able to reflect more effectively on what has happened in your day and how you are developing as a person. It also gives you the time and space to contemplate; you may use meditation to reflect on a teaching or question that you have. For example, if you have been impatient during the day, you may wish to meditate and reflect on how developing patience may be of benefit to you and how it might remove some of your own obstacles to happiness. By contemplating patience during your meditation you will be more ready to practise it during your everyday life.

If you start to meditate today, for the first time, you may not find it very easy or even very helpful to begin with, as while you are trying to reflect on patience your mind will be running around all over the place. But be patient with your meditation – see, there is even a lesson in how difficult it is to begin with. And then gradually, *if you keep doing it*, after a week or two, you will eventually be able to do it very easily with no difficulties.

Our minds need to be relaxed and peaceful for this to happen, which is why we chant mantras and then meditate; the rhythm of singing the mantras creates a relaxation, for me it is like swimming in the deep ocean. In this relaxed state we can gradually develop a feeling of space in our minds so that there is room for understanding and inspiration rather than the usual mass of nonsense thoughts clamouring for our attention.

MINDFULNESS

Many people tend to think of meditation as specific practices that they might do at the beginning or end of the day. However, to truly understand how the mind is the creator of everything and how we might infuse our whole life with a deeper sense of happiness, we need to bring the art of meditation into the rest of our day.

Today, this is called 'mindfulness'. It's something that has been taught throughout the ages, not just by Buddha but by many philosophers and spiritual leaders. And now, science too is giving us clues as to how we can help ourselves and each other when it comes to happiness.

I tend to describe mindfulness as simply *being in your life*. By paying attention and raising your awareness you bring yourself into the present moment. If you can strip away some of the complications and misunderstandings that hamper your ability to get on with things with passion and drive, then you can instead bring your attention right here into the moment with curiosity and engagement.

Make mindfulness a habit

Mindfulness is more than just being aware of things; it is the ability to maintain a calm and steady awareness of body, speech and mind, yet it is free of judgments, concepts and self-references. It is both a practice and a state of mind. Mindfulness needs to become a habit, so that your entire life, moment to moment, every breath is full of awareness and clarity.

Generally, we develop mindfulness in stages – mindfulness of body first, followed by the mindfulness of feelings, of consciousness and lastly, of the nature of existence or phenomena.

- **Mindfulness of body** means seeing the body as a physical form without any ego-clinging attachment – so seeing the body as it is, without the label of 'my' or 'I'. When we are mindful of the body, in particular the natural rhythm of our breathing, we help to tame the 'monkey mind' that swings from one thought to the next. We are able to pause.
- **Mindfulness of feelings** or sensations means recognising your emotions and seeing them as separate entities. Do not let emotions define who you are. This helps to acknowledge our emotions and deal with them.

51

- **Mindfulness of consciousness** is to observe your mind and thoughts; do not form any judgments and ideas. You will recognise the thought patterns, how one thought flows to the next and chases after the next.

- **Mindfulness of the nature of existence** recognises the relationship between ourselves and the external world. This helps us to understand that everything is inter-dependent – and this understanding is the basis of developing wisdom: nothing appears as it seems to be, everything is relative and interdependent on something else. For example, in order to understand heat, we have to experience cold; so coldness needs to be there for heat to be experienced. Do we know where our food comes from? Are we aware of where our water comes from? If we are mindful of these little things in the nature of existence, we would also realise that our own existence depends on others. This is the first step to the development of greater wisdom, greater love, greater kindness and greater compassion. Mindfulness helps us become the person we want to be.

Everyday mindfulness opens you up to new experiences and points of view, so that you are willing to learn from others and enjoy the possibility of seeing things differently. You no longer rely on the old labels you used to use to interpret the world. You immerse yourself in the journey of life, no longer fixated on the outcome or the destination.

Along with mindfulness and meditation, feel free to let your mind wander too, to let your imagination go free without the usual limitations of self-beliefs and labels. Create a balance between using meditation to sharpen your focus and simply to take a mental breather. You are the best judge of whether your mind needs a workout or a rest.

Meditation in practice

Sometimes people worry when they are a beginner that they might not get everything 'right'. But we are really all beginners, even those of us who have been practising for many years. So never worry and know that there is no right or wrong way to meditate; it is simply a guiding process to help you get to know yourself and develop your understanding.

Meditation posture

There are seven features of the basic posture:

1. Cross-legged, with the left leg inside.
2. Straight back.
3. Shoulders stretched straight, like the wings of an eagle.
4. Neck slightly bent.
5. Eyes open, focused and downcast to about one metre in front.

6. Mouth slightly open with the tip of the tongue touching the upper palate.
7. Hands on lap, right palm over the left, with thumbs gently touching.

You can engage in meditation anywhere – while sitting in a chair, standing or walking. However, by sitting to meditate in the position described your body is grounded, which will help to ground your mind. The main point to remember is to keep your chest and shoulders open, so that you may draw in your breath deeply and by keeping your body posture open you will help to open up your mind.

Breathing meditation

For this meditation on the breath, keep your posture straight and follow the sequence below:

1. Gently close the right nostril with a finger and take in a long, deep breath through the left nostril.
2. Hold the breath at the end of the inhale for a few seconds.
3. Close the left nostril, open the right one and breathe out of it.
4. Now breathe in through the right nostril, keeping the left closed. Hold at the end of the inhale and then exhale through the left nostril.

5. Next, gently breathe in through both nostrils at the same time. Breathe out with some force now to get as much air out as possible.

White light, black smoke meditation

Here, while breathing in, we visualise that all the positivity of the world enters into us in the form of a white light. When breathing out, we visualise that all the negativity inside us – like anger, jealousy or sadness – comes out in the form of a black smoke.

1. Begin with a long exhalation through both nostrils – visualise all the anger, hatred, negative karma, disappointment and stress coming out in the form of black smoke.
2. Close the left nostril with your finger, inhale deeply through the right nostril and keep it in the stomach for two seconds – visualise all the positivity going into your body in the form of white light.
3. Then, close the right nostril; exhale all the negativity through the left nostril in the form of black smoke.
4. Inhale one more time all the positive thoughts through the left nostril in the form of white light.
5. Close your left nostril and exhale all the negative thoughts through your right nostril in the form of black smoke.

6. Inhale deeply all the good and positive thoughts with both nostrils in the form of white light.
7. Exhale with slight force all the bad and negative thoughts through both nostrils in the form of black smoke.

This is one set. It is usually done in three sets or more, if you like.

Focus-on-the-body meditation

Allow your mind to take care of your body for the duration of this meditation, giving your body a chance to deeply relax and feel bathed by your appreciation for it:

- Start by lying down on the back, either on your bed or on the floor. Close your eyes and let your arms rest gently in a natural position by your sides. Allow your legs to rest and relax, falling slightly outwards.

- As you breathe in and out, down below your diaphragm, sense all the places where your body is touching the floor or the bed, and with each breath allow yourself to sink further down through these places of contact so that you feel heavy and grounded. Focus only on your body, letting go of your tension, your worries, your hopes and your fears.

- Bring your focus to your breath and notice the rise and fall of your abdomen as you breathe in, and breathe out.

- After a few breaths, bring your focus down to your toes. You might like to imagine breathing in white, positive energy and focusing that energy on your feet. Really explore your sensations and imagine your feet happy and relaxed. Release all the tension.

- Now, bring your focus up your legs, slowly, to your calves, your knees and your thighs. If you have any pain, send your love and good energy to the point of pain and allow yourself to relax.

- Bring your awareness to all the different parts of your body; take a few breaths to focus on your hands, being thankful for all the creativity and care they hold within them.

- Be aware of your organs, as well as your limbs. Bring your focus to your heart, being thankful for its incredible ability to never take a break and for the beating that is the rhythm of your life. Be thankful for your stomach that gives you nourishment and vitality from the food you eat. Your eyes give you a chance to see this beautiful world, from the deep blue of the vast ocean to the love you see reflected in your partner's eyes. Your ears allow you to listen, so that you might be a good friend; they give you the chance to hear a child's laughter or hear the birds sing at dawn. You are able to taste delicious foods through your mouth and speak with grace, sharing your happiness with those around you, teaching and inspiring others, constantly learning through interaction and connection. With your nose you are able to appreciate the scent of a flower, freshly baked bread, just-cut grass, the early beginnings of spring when you realise you can smell the earth waking up after the long sleep of winter.

- Send your strength, your love and your appreciation to all parts of your body, especially if you have any pain or if you are unwell.

- And for the last part of the meditation, bring your awareness to your whole body: relax in the sensation of sinking down into the bed or the floor. Send out your appreciation with every breath and, as you do so, gently bring your focus back to the rise and fall of your abdomen once again, just for the last couple of breaths.

Slowly open your eyes, you might wiggle your toes or have a gentle stretch before you get up. Keep your movements relaxed and calm. Carry your calm and your gratitude with you for the rest of the day.

LIFE IS YOUR MEDITATION

To see a world in a grain of sand
And a heaven in a wild flower
Hold infinity in the palm of your hand
And eternity in an hour.

WILLIAM BLAKE, AUGURIES OF INNOCENCE

In 2012, I was invited to visit the Oxford Mindfulness Centre and while there I met Mark Williams, who does great work on mindfulness and its modern-day applications. He is doing an amazing job of bringing an ancient practice into the mainstream. One thing in particular that Mark said which caught my immediate attention was that while most people have a map, they don't walk the journey. This is a great truth! We are all equipped with all sorts of information – in fact, I think we are actually 'overdosed' with information – but we don't experientially understand it. So we learn about things through books or classes, but we don't take the next step of living them.

Life is the best teacher of all, so the more attentive we are to *how* we are actually going through it and experiencing it, the more chance we have of learning about and developing ourselves. So if we want to bring more joy into life, all we need to do is look a little more closely at it; and if we want to find the meaning of life, all we need to do is let ourselves really live it, to embrace our fears and our uncertainties and jump in.

Some people have the perception that if we concern ourselves with the minute details of our day – say, the enjoyment of a cup of tea or doing the washing up – then we might miss out on the bigger picture or greater opportunities for happiness. But from my point of view, it is being aware enough to take delight in a cup of tea that opens us up to the possibilities of life – we will enjoy the journey, rather than allow ourselves only a glimpse of happiness once we reach the destination. We will become better watchers of ourselves and our minds, so that we will begin to understand where unhappiness and mental sufferings come from, the roots of our impatience, jealousies and our anger. We will discover that we have a great deal more time in the day than we realised, but at the same time remember that life is short, so why not be happy?

The following chapters contain the tools that will help you to cultivate a happy state of mind; to uncover and embrace your true inner nature – one that is beautiful, confident, active, engaged and in the flow of life. There are 'mindful meditations' throughout that you can put into practice to help you create habits of happiness. They remind you to be grateful for everything you already have in your life, to be friendly with all your emotions, so that you may be less attached to them, to share your happiness and to be present, so that you may reconnect with yourself, with those around you and with the world.

Part II

Cultivating a
Happy State of Mind

As you start to walk out on the way,
the way appears.
RUMI

The Buddha said that wisdom and compassion are like the two wings of a bird; it is only when you have both, working in union together, that you can fly.

In modern terms, we can also think of wisdom and compassion as understanding and action. At the heart of all the teachings is the aim to develop the union between our thoughts, our words and our actions. Everything begins and is created first in the mind, but if we don't put our understanding into action, then we forget to walk our path. The chapters in this part of the book – the essence of which is summed up below – provide the tools that help us to connect with ourselves, our world and our happiness.

CHOOSE HAPPINESS

There are things in this life that we can't change or that we can't control, but whether we want to experience happiness or not is up to us. If we don't wish to be happier than we are now, that is our choice, but if we wish to deepen our sense of happiness, to become a more joyful person to be around, then the first step is to set our intention and *choose happiness over suffering*. It sounds like a simple choice, but it is easy to become used to low-level suffering and wonder whether it will be worth the effort to reach beyond our familiar *dis*comfort zone and into less-known territory.

BE GRATEFUL

Happiness is our nature. It's right here, right now, but we need to remind ourselves to *notice* it in our lives, rather than go chasing after it. Gratitude shines a light on our happiness within; it stills the turbulent surface of our minds and encourages us to pause and reflect for a moment on all the things that we already have – the things that we hold in our hands ready to make a happy and fulfilling life. It is like diving beneath the waves to discover the beauty of the deep ocean, where there is a whole other world of coral and fish and life that we couldn't see from above. Appreciation begins to help us develop other happiness skills like patience. We remind ourselves to be joyful about all the good things in our lives, rather than envious of others or fixated on acquiring what we don't have. Appreciation helps us to make the most of today, and to be less anxious about tomorrow.

FREE YOUR MIND TO BE HAPPY

We were born with limitless imaginations, and then over time we construct a web of beliefs and opinions that become filters through which we see and colour the world. We impose conditions and restrictions on happiness, believing it to be a limited resource, and so we end up limiting our own potential, labelling ourselves and others as one thing or the other. This is the work of the ego, which likes to put everything in boxes. We become so attached to our sense of identity that our minds begin to become quite small and inflexible, and rather than adapt to situations or people we tend to suffer instead with irritation, impatience, even anger. As soon as we can be a little looser and understand that there is always potential for change, we free our minds to open up and let so much more happiness in.

CHANGE YOUR MENTAL HABITS

Our perceptions shape our reality. It is with our minds that we create our world and our place in it. We get very used to seeing things our way, and we don't really like it when people or circumstances around us don't conform to our view of how things should be. We believe that others are making us unhappy, or things that happen to us ruin our chances for happiness, but if we give ourselves the opportunity for reflection, we can begin to watch our minds and see how they work. Once we begin to understand that our thoughts form our sense of reality, we can appreciate how the potential for transformation originates in the way we think about life and what we are going to do today to make a better tomorrow.

EMBRACE YOUR FEARS

However much we might try to cling to the shores of certainty in our lives, life is by its very nature a great unknown; we don't know what is going to happen next and the not knowing can become the seed of fear in our minds. Equally, we may use our pain and suffering from the past to influence how we think about the future: if things have gone wrong before, we may expect them to go wrong again. As we begin to practise choosing happiness, freeing our minds to be happy, seeing things differently and appreciating every day, we might see our fears and uncertainties from an alternative angle. We begin to see that where there is fear there is life and where there is uncertainty there will be things that surprise and delight us.

BE FRIENDLY WITH ALL YOUR EMOTIONS

Life is full of ups and downs, and our emotions are our signposts. We mustn't hide them away, therefore, especially if we would like to understand such difficult emotions as anger or jealousy and work with ourselves to experience these negative states less often. We need to make friends with all our emotions, both positive and negative, so that we can begin to see where they come from or how they are triggered. And the more friendly we are with even the most painful emotions, the more easily we can let them go. As we practise the tools of patience, appreciation, understanding the nature of change and acceptance, we will gradually find that our emotions may become friendlier towards us. As we become better observers of our minds through meditation and everyday mindfulness, we may feel the burn of anger dissolve before the fire has even got going.

STOP COMPARING

We live in an era of competition and comparison, and while competition is one way to drive us to greater heights, it also develops in our minds the idea of winners and losers, creating anxiety about where we are on some imaginary ladder of success, achievement or even happiness relative to others. So instead of being happy for another person's success or happiness, we look upon them with jealousy and envy; or if we are very successful ourselves, we might be full of pride, looking down on others from a supposed great height. This chapter is dedicated to putting all of our comparisons, gossip and judgments about others aside, while we focus on being true to ourselves, without the need for praise or blame.

DEVELOP MEANINGFUL CONNECTIONS

It is when we interact with the world and make connections that we open up opportunities to give and receive happiness, inspiration, teachings, kindness and love. And the more that we develop our connections with the world, the more beauty we will see in life; they will nourish and support us when we need them and give us so many wonderful ideas and moments and experiences. We must learn to be great listeners, cultivate our patience, be willing students of life and never be afraid to reach out.

ALLOW YOUR HEART TO BE BROKEN

To experience all of our emotions fully, even to allow our hearts to be broken, is to allow ourselves to be vulnerable and therefore truly experience life. It is only by understanding suffering that we truly understand happiness.

GIVE TODAY YOUR FULL ATTENTION

The best way to be happy is to go ahead and be happy today. Don't put it off. Don't wait for all the conditions to be perfect. Don't let the rain put you off . . . Bring your mind and your body into the moment and fully experience your day. Switch off the autopilot and really notice the detail. Build on all the good things and, if there are things that you would like to change in your life, start small and start today.

There is no time like the present to be happy.

5

Choose Happiness

*And when the night grows dark, when injustice
weighs heavily on our hearts or our best-laid plans
seem beyond our reach – think of Madiba, and
the words that brought him comfort within the four
walls of a cell: 'It matters not how strait the gate,
How charged with punishments the scroll, I am the
master of my fate: I am the captain of my soul.'*

BARACK OBAMA AT THE MEMORIAL SERVICE

FOR NELSON MANDELA

As Mandela believed, even within the confines of the walls of a prison cell, we are the masters of our own fate, because we are the masters of our own minds. Whatever obstacles we come across in life, our nature remains constant. It is our essence, our strength that we may nourish in good times and draw on when we need support.

Choosing happiness is like flicking a light switch, bringing into focus all the things you have in this life to be appreciative of. You may not feel you have much of a choice in many aspects of your life, but the number of choices and opportunities available today can be overwhelming. With so many decisions to make you can sometimes forget that you also get to choose whether you are happy or not. You might get so caught up in worrying about whether you will make the right or wrong choices that you start to put off making decisions altogether, sheltering in the comfort of the status quo whether you like it very much or not.

In reality, the only thing standing in the way of your happiness is you; the only thing holding you back is your mind, and it is your mind that can equally help you to see your happiness, to let it colour your day and your life. But like your body, your mind needs a good workout to be fit and flexible, to release the tension of irritation and impatience. You need to give yourself the space in which to look at your mind openly and honestly, and be willing to let go of your suffering, your old resentments and your anxieties about the future. None of these things is doing you a service, but in their familiarity they can almost become comfortable – because if you let down your barriers, who knows what might happen? There might be an even bigger hurt or a failure waiting for you; you just don't know if it's worth the risk.

People have a hard time letting go of their suffering. Out of a fear of the unknown, they prefer suffering that is familiar. THICH NHAT HANH

Choosing happiness today gives us no guarantees as to what will happen tomorrow; but actually, none of our safety mechanisms give us guarantees – all they do is limit us and prevent us from really living. If we begin to look after our minds and allow ourselves to *be ourselves*, however, we will have the strength and the flexibility to choose happiness even while accepting that life is full of ups and downs. This is authentic living, and when we are authentic our happiness shines through, even if today is a rainy day, even if our boss ignores us or somebody bumps into us. The more we choose happiness, the more strength and courage we develop for those times in our lives when we feel brought to our knees by grief, sorrow or pain; the more we choose happiness, the more clear we become in our intentions – we begin to know the meaning of our lives, we notice the detail and instead of taking so much for granted, and wanting so much more, we are able to sit and see the beauty in everything we have.

Man is fully responsible for his nature and his choices.
JEAN-PAUL SARTRE

You get to say what is important in your life, what brings you happiness, and it's up to you to choose to do those things and be with those people more on a daily basis. You might be afraid that if you choose happiness today then it may be taken away from you tomorrow, but you always get to choose because your happiness depends only on you.

Our inflexibility, the fear of stepping out of our comfort zones and the habit of giving ourselves excuses can be the main reasons for our unhappiness and our failures. My wish is to help those who are connected with me to break free from all these nonsense concepts and to be free. You cannot make others happy when you are not happy. Whether you are happy or not, it's entirely up to you. You are your own boss!

Finding happiness within

For Kirsty, it was through a combination of experience and contemplation – living meditation – that she realised she could stop chasing happiness and discover it within:

I remember at the age of sixteen, I wrote about Buddhism for a school project. It was the highest grade I had ever received for religious studies. There was something about Buddha's words and teachings that touched my heart and mind so deeply; perhaps it was because the words were so liberating that I got top marks.

Many years later, when I listened to teachings given by His Holiness Gyalwang Drukpa, I realised that for a long time I had been searching outside of myself for my healing and my happiness. I had tried many things in my spiritual and personal quest. For example I had tried yoga, chi kung, giving up meat,

71

caffeine, wine, all those things. I looked for happiness in love and in moving to new places in which to live. All the time I was trying to fill a vacuum with things outside of me, when all along everything I needed was within.

I remember as I sat and listened to the teachings and the wisdom of this old philosophy, I began to have the first inkling of understanding that opened my mind to an alternative truth about reality. I felt that I was beginning to find out about the nature of the mind, and the power of the mind to help and to heal.

I had searched outside of myself and now all I had to do was find the Buddha within. Now, after ten plus years, I am so much more aware of how my mind creates my reality, and so when I am confronted with loss, sorrow, hurt and pain I use the tools of the teachings and this gentle spiritual philosophy to place me in the safe and kindest of states one could rest in.

Of course, the process of trying to practise forgiveness, compassion, patience and all those things is a wisdom that is a continuous daily learning process. The more I do it, by putting intentions into practice, I find the more I enjoy it; it is an ongoing living meditation.

HOW DO YOU LOOK AT THE WORLD?

Don't cry because it's over. Smile because it happened. DR SEUSS

I would not deny that we all have tendencies when it comes to our personalities; some of us will incline to be more adventurous than others, more optimistic or more fearful. But by leaving it there we are doing ourselves a great disservice – because however much of our sense of self is inherited from our parents or imprinted at a young age and then again as we go through life's experiences, I also believe that when we allow our minds to go beneath the surface of inheritance or experience, we have the possibility to discover our inner nature.

Some people may even write themselves off to a lesser or greater degree by describing themselves as a 'generally pessimistic' person, for example; but if they expect the worst, then perhaps the reality might come as a nice surprise once in a while. A woman I met in London told me a little story that illustrates this perfectly. She was visiting one of London's wonderful museums with her good friend. As they were leaving, having had a very enjoyable time, she spotted the most incredible glass sculpture hanging above the circular reception area of the museum. 'Wow, look at that!' she exclaimed, pointing the sculpture out to her friend, who instantly replied, 'I wouldn't want to walk underneath that. If it fell, you'd be dead instantly.' The two women looked at each other and burst out laughing. The friend had the sense of humour and sense of self to see immediately what she had done: 'Oh dear,' she said. 'That just about sums the two of us up: there you are marvelling at a piece of art and I immediately see the potential for disaster!' The first step to any change is being aware of the need or desire for it. By understanding that they had both seen the exact same thing from different perspectives the woman's friend took a great step towards awareness of the power of the mind. And while it might not happen overnight, it is possible to use such moments of awareness as a foundation for training the mind to begin to see things differently – to *choose* another point of view.

It is very important that we wake ourselves up from the habitual comfort of pessimistic or negative thoughts and acknowledge that such thinking is a choice, rather than something we shrug our shoulders about and write off as just the way we are. If we don't give our courage a chance to show itself, then we don't allow ourselves to flourish and take leaps of faith. And simply on the level of our day-to-day lives, we don't give ourselves the chance to see the beauty that is all around us, focusing instead on the potential pitfalls. Of course, when we choose to look up at the sky and the trees and the smiles of other people, instead of constantly checking for cracks in the pavement, occasionally we might trip up and feel a little foolish. But when we are choosing happiness we can also laugh at ourselves, even if we fall right on our bottoms. As Oprah Winfrey says: 'So go ahead. Fall down. The world looks different from the ground.'

RELAX INTO YOUR NATURE

I am told that in America rates of happiness are decreasing despite its being one of the richest countries on the planet. The number of people who describe themselves as optimists has fallen by a quarter in just a few years, while wealth has increased. This shows just how much people's minds can change – it's easy to believe that we must be born either an optimist or a pessimist but this trend shows how it is possible to change from one to another. Sadly, in America, more people have become increasingly negative in their outlook, but fortunately science is now discovering how practices like meditation can help people to have a more positive outlook. I believe that if people can stop looking outside of themselves to the things they cannot control for their happiness and instead realise that all the conditions exist within them, they can be optimists even when times are a little harder.

Of course, life is full of ups and downs – it is quite a winding and bumpy road for most of us with good times and sad or challenging times; but perhaps it is possible to remain strong at the foundation – like a tree that has strong roots while also being able to bend and be flexible even in pretty high winds. Can we walk a middle path of balance, so that we may understand how wonderful this life is both when things are externally going well for us as well as when things are not so good?

Renewed confidence

I have had the pleasure to know Suman's family for many years, and feel very supported by them in so many ways. When Suman lost his way a few years ago it was my privilege to be a guide as he found his own way back to his path:

I am from India and my mother was Sikh and my father was Hindu. I lived with my father's parents and I was often taken to both Hindu and Sikh temples, so religion was a way of life for me from a young age. And then along came this Buddhist master; I remember His Holiness and his parents coming to stay with us from when I was a child and that I felt very happy to be around them.

One of the biggest lessons for me was to watch the respect between His Holiness and his parents. His father was also a Rinpoche and great teacher; his mother was love and compassion in human form. I hope that the way he takes care of his parents rubbed off on me subconsciously.

As a young adult, I really began to struggle with my motivation. My parents had become successful and I had become very lazy. I was working in a high-salaried job with an oil company, but inside I was miserable and I didn't want to work any more. I became depressed and the doctors prescribed medication for me, but it wasn't working. I was at my wits' end with insomnia and couldn't see a way forward.

Luckily, I went to see His Holiness at this time. He gave me a specific meditation to practise and said that I wasn't to take any pills that night. His total belief in me gave me the belief I needed, and so I meditated and for the first night in months I slept soundly. We also talked about how I had lost my motivation to work and His Holiness helped me to see things from a completely new perspective. He said that if I didn't want the money for myself, then why not make it for the nuns? He said that if I just sat around, how could I help him! I suddenly realised that money isn't a bad thing – it's your relationship with it that can either be positive or negative. It was entirely up to me how I chose to see money, and whether I wanted to see the good that it could bring with the right intentions and motivation. His Holiness simply shone a light on the fact that there was choice. There is always a choice.

I discovered what mutual respect means in that moment. His Holiness showed me that he had confidence in my nature – that despite my sinking into the depths of a mental depression, there remained an inner strength and that I had just forgotten its existence and so needed a little help to get back to my senses. His Holiness asks for nothing in return, but my respect for him deepened very much during this exchange. His trust in me and his fierce compassion inspired my own trust in him as well as a renewed confidence in myself.

Intention meditation

In the Buddhist teachings, we have an aspiration prayer, which is a *wishing* prayer. Like all the teachings, this is something we think about to help us develop ourselves and live the Dharma, which is just to say living life. This meditation encourages us to look into our hearts, find the inspiration and generate the motivation to turn our wishes – or our thoughts – into actions. In other words, we need to aspire first, then engage, so that we may apply our intentions to what we do. In this way we unify our thoughts, words and actions; we unify our minds, our hearts and our bodies. And it all begins with the mind: the creator of everything.

In this short meditation, therefore, we keep things very simple and just take a few minutes to set our intention and generate our motivation, like restarting our computer first thing in the morning.

1. You can sit in the meditation posture as described on page 53, or just sit comfortably in a chair.
2. Bring your attention into the present by practising the Breathing Meditation (see p. 54) for a couple of minutes.
3. Now bring your thoughts to the people in your life – those who support you and care for you and those who are more challenging. Focus in this moment on your love and compassion for *all* the people in your life and those who you may come into contact with today.

4. Focus on the intention that you would like all your thoughts, words and actions today to be of help to others, to inspire or teach, to be patient and understanding.
5. Now focus simply on the intention that today you will do your best in whatever tasks or interactions you have.

It might help you to read the following sentences, which are a simple mantra, and then close your eyes to bring yourself into your mind and focus on what they mean to you:

- May I set my intention to be considerate of and to help those people around me today – my loved ones, my colleagues, all the people I happen to interact with during my day.
- We are all in the same boat. We all hope to be happy and free from suffering. Whatever our differences, we are also the same.
- Today, I will do my best.

FREEDOM THROUGH DISCIPLINE

Happiness is a choice that requires effort at times.
AESCHYLUS

Creating a new habit or practice, such as meditation or mindfulness, takes patience and discipline – it requires a commitment to change because we know that it will be worth it. Any kind of action that calls for discipline is difficult at the start – our minds are experts at resistance and creating many excuses why we shouldn't bother to change. But never be frightened of change; to make a change is to be inspired. Don't be frightened to learn, to improve – because if you feed your inspiration, you will, in turn, inspire others, and that is a great gift. When we are inspired we become so much more aware, we can be spontaneous and make decisions boldly and swiftly.

In Sanskrit, the word for discipline is *shila*, which means 'cooling'; when you feel very hot in your mind or emotions *shila* is like a fan that cools you down and relaxes you. You know the feeling when you (or, in other words, 'your mind') are getting out of control, and you know that to help yourself you need discipline. For example, if you realise that you have got into the habit of eating too much and so you have been putting on weight; what was once a pleasure is no longer a source of happiness, but rather a craving or even a source of negative emotions like guilt. This is when you need genuine discipline to break the habit and become slim and healthy again.

Often, when you first decide to make a change it is very hard and not enjoyable at all. But if you can keep going, by checking your intention and finding ways to motivate and inspire yourself, you will reach a point where the discipline becomes like *shila* – a freshness in the mind, a moment of true realisation, when you know you are doing something that is good for yourself, and you really feel it in your heart, as well as knowing it in your mind.

This is why taking care of the mind is so important. It's impossible to effect a change – like eating more healthily, for example – if we do not also address what is going on in our thoughts, exploring them so that we can discover our genuine inspiration for change. It is hard to put things into practice, if we are not in the right frame of mind. So we remind ourselves of how great a gift life is to us. We ask: why do we make ourselves sick in the body and mind through eating so many things that are not good for us? We realise how fortunate we are to have the choice of what we can eat each day, and remember that we have the opportunity to eat foods that will nourish our bodies, to exercise and increase our strength and physical fitness. And when we combine a good attitude with healthy action, the sum becomes even greater than the parts, each nourishing the other.

So happiness springs from a healthy attitude. We begin to understand that happiness is no longer contingent on external factors and that our own minds hold the key to uncovering what is there inside. Milarepa, the Tibetan poet and saint, said, 'My religion is to live – and die – without regret.' These few words contain the aspirations of all of us, I think: to live our lives well, to be brave and make the most of our time, to be happy.

Choose-happiness reminders

- The only person who gets to choose whether you are happy is you.

- You can always choose happiness, because happiness is your nature.

- In choosing happiness, you develop resilience for the times in your life when you feel brought to your knees.

- How would you like to look at the world? It's up to you.

- Don't be afraid of falling down; just know that you have the courage to stand up where you fall.

- Set your intention each day.

A Random Act of Happiness

Smile at a passerby: a smile changes your whole face, your posture and your attitude. It is even contagious: when the brain sees a smile we can't help but want to smile back. Smiling is like a happiness switch for the mind, with the power to evaporate a bad mood in an instant.

6

Be Grateful

Subjected to so many ills, life
is even more impermanent
Than a water bubble which the wind
threatens to burst.
Thus, how extraordinary to inhale before exhaling!
To awaken after dozing.

SUHLLEKHA

While we are busy complaining and looking for
reasons to dislike or be angry with our circumstances
and the people around us, we still expect ourselves
to be happy. But if our minds are only looking for
problems, how can we be? If gratitude and appreciation are lacking in our lives, we will miss the path to
happiness.

WHAT IS GOING WELL IN YOUR LIFE?

Actual happiness always looks pretty squalid in
comparison with the overcompensations for misery.
And, of course, stability isn't nearly so spectacular
as instability. And being contented has none of the

glamour of a good fight against misfortune, none of the picturesqueness of a struggle with temptation, or a fatal overthrow by passion or doubt. Happiness is never grand. ALDOUS HUXLEY, BRAVE NEW WORLD

People often tend to focus on what is going wrong in their lives, rather than giving themselves a chance to dwell on what's going well. It is true that we can learn very helpful lessons from things that happen which we would describe as mistakes. And learning such lessons allows us to develop our skills, our compassion and the ability to see things from alternative points of view. However, sometimes I think we forget there are great lessons to be had from the parts of life that fill us with joy. Simply the act of shining a light on those good feelings encourages them to grow and infuse the rest of our life, or at least the rest of our day.

Why not celebrate and develop the things we do well? We can't all be good at everything, and while it's no bad idea to challenge ourselves and look for new areas in which we can learn, we can also hone the skills we have been blessed with. After all, they then become gifts with which we can improve other people's lives in some way. When we feel like we are a very good fit with what we are doing – whether that is in our job, our relationship or any other aspect of life – we don't need to spend so much time looking around the next corner for happiness because we feel it in our contentment and our relaxed confidence. When we get back to the simplicity of doing something well, we are lucky enough to remind ourselves of the essence of life.

We seem to find it much easier to believe in the negative side of things (this is where our belief is at its strongest) and we have no confidence in the good things. But to change life in the positive sense, let's start with believing that happiness, joy, peace – all the great things – can happen with us first. We can be fearless if we want to.

So we might wake up in the morning and think for a few moments about the loving people in our lives, that we have a roof over our heads, a cup of tea first thing and the ingredients in our cupboards for a good breakfast. We then think about the things we are grateful for that we don't have today: illness, for example, if we are in good health, blindness, if we can see, homelessness, if we have a home. This kind of thinking not only helps to bring our happiness to the surface, but also to tune in our awareness. As we train our minds to consider the things in our lives that make us want to say 'thank you', we begin to notice more of them and take fewer things for granted. The other benefit is that by practising this kind of thinking we also help to develop our compassion for others; we are able to acknowledge suffering and have the strength to look directly at it, so that we may also have the motivation to help those in need.

Thank-you tonic

Since listening to His Eminence Gyalwa Dokhampa (a spiritual son of His Holiness the Gyalwang Drukpa), I have been writing my thank yous every day and it has been so helpful for encouraging my positive state of mind. I have been poorly with a bad cough and ear infection, and my husband has been struggling to walk with a painful ankle. We are a feeling like a right couple of old souls, but taking the time to remember each day all of the lovely things in our lives has been like taking a tonic.

WORK ON YOUR STRENGTHS

Don't be afraid that appreciation for what is present in your life right now will somehow stop you from striving or being ambitious. To be content and appreciative is not to be confused with being complacent. If you can hold gratitude in your heart and mind, you can begin to live in the present, rather than wishing for the good old days of the past or putting off happiness as something you will only allow yourself as a reward for some outstanding goal or desire. You continue to create goals and to strive, but you also allow yourself to recognise the positive things in your life right now, today. The more you work on your strengths, the bigger the contribution that you will make to the world and to all the people around you. By turning your mind around in this way, you give

nourishment to those good things – your loving relationships, for example – and they begin to bloom in
even more beautiful ways.

Even those who are a little more on the pessimistic
than optimistic side of the scales can begin to see
what's right in front of them with appreciation, rather
than spending so many of their thoughts on worrying
about things in the future. Likewise, if you are
someone who is very optimistic, but always running
towards the next project, or if you can't wait for the
next turning along your path, you can use this sense
of appreciating your life right now to bring you back
into the present moment, so you can enjoy today as
much as the thought of tomorrow.

PUT ASIDE YOUR COMPLAINTS

*Man only likes to count his troubles; he doesn't
calculate his happiness.*
FYODOR DOSTOYEVSKY, *NOTES FROM UNDERGROUND*

When we develop our appreciation of every day we
begin to be able to let go of our ideas of perfection
– the 'if onlys': this present my husband gave me for
our anniversary is lovely, but if only he'd thought to
take me out for dinner; this job is challenging and
exciting – if only my boss weren't so moody, I could
really enjoy it . . .

Sometimes I think we make life very complicated
for ourselves. We go the long way round in our search

of happiness or inspiration when it's right there, with us all the time. I can see why this happens though. Just turn on the news and you'll think nothing ever good happens in the world – all you see and hear is bad news, sad news and violent news. Then you start to believe that the only way to get a bit of attention yourself is to act like a drama king or queen; you may find yourself saying things like, 'You think your day was bad, listen to mine'. Think how much more happiness you could have if you banished all the complaints in your thoughts, at least for a few minutes of the day!

I have met many people on my travels who have taught me some incredible lessons about appreciating every day. People who have been initially devastated by the diagnosis of a serious condition will often let go of all the small complaints they'd normally find themselves making and see the gift of life with a new sense of clarity. It might sound morbid, but when we truly accept the certainty of death we truly appreciate life. This is why Buddhist teachings encourage people to reflect on death, rather than hide it away in the corners of their minds. If we don't accept today that we might die, at any moment, then how will we really live? And instead of fearing death, we can use this one certainty in our lives to inspire us to release all the conditions we place on happiness. There is no need to put off happiness; you can allow it into your mind and your heart today.

Below is an excerpt from my own diary, from the

Eco Pad Yatra to Sri Lanka, a country torn apart by war but where we found joy and appreciation every step of the way. The Eco Pad Yatras are 'walking pilgrimages' that we organise each year with hundreds of nuns, monks and volunteers, so that we can visit remote villages while picking up all the plastic waste we find along the way.

Besides the warm hospitality that we received throughout our one-month walk from the south to the north of Sri Lanka, we were moved to witness the possible harmony among different religions and races. Whenever we passed through pockets of Muslim and Hindu areas, we were offered shelters, food, drinks and prayers. No one came with an angry face whenever hundreds of us walked through their towns, villages and holy places. For a country that had gone through three decades of violent war, it was very difficult for me to believe that the people could continue their life with smiles and forgiveness. We walked from south to north and it wouldn't be easy for the government or the people to hide any negative happening from us. We were free to interact with anyone. I asked many people why were they able to keep themselves free of pain after what they had gone through. Most of them gave credit to the Buddhist monks who gave teaching on karma, appreciation, tolerance and forgiveness. I know that many of my friends and students have doubts in the teachings, and especially in karma, but we all could see in Sri Lanka how important Dharma was for the people who were going through thirty years of war. Parents had to tell their children every morning before going to work that they might not return – they could be killed in terrorist attacks. They told their children that they had to follow the teachings of the Buddha and continue living with love, patience and understanding, because it would come a time when the negative karma is exhausted, peace would prevail again. This is the effect of putting Dharma into practice.

With an eye made quiet by the power of harmony, and the deep power of joy, we see into the life of things. WILLIAM WORDSWORTH

'Thank-you' meditation

In America the Thanksgiving holiday is as significant as Christmas Day, if not more so, perhaps, as it is celebrated by many faiths and communities. Being thankful is really the best tool we have for bringing happiness to the surface of our minds. So don't wait to be thankful for one day in the year – give yourself a few minutes every day to remind yourself of the things in your life for which you can say thank you.

Each morning when you wake up, spend a few moments thinking about everything you have to feel good about in your life:

- Think of the people closest to you.

- Think of your body and be thankful for your senses and the health you have.

- Think of the things that you are happy not to have in your life, such as illness or homelessness.

- Think of what has inspired you recently.

- Think about the good parts of your work.

This exercise encourages you to look both inwards and outwards. It is a simple but powerful reminder of the riches you have in your life already. You might be thankful for your health, the roof over your head, the fact that today might be an interesting or fun day. And as you mentally say thank you to your loved ones, you may find that you tend to focus more on their good points and that this, in turn, will encourage you to show your happiness towards them through being thoughtful and caring and asking what they need as a way of saying thanks for being in your life.

It is easy to get caught up with analysing what we need to fix or change in our lives; to turn such questions over and over in our minds. We worry a great deal about the things that might go wrong, while forgetting to nurture and enjoy all the things that are already going right. And if we can practise saying thanks every day when we are generally feeling ok, it will stand us in good stead when we are faced with more difficult times. The habits of happiness that we will develop will give us an underlying strength and resilience.

When you practise this very short meditation daily your whole outlook on life begins to be easier, happier. It is the best way to get out of bed on the right side.

Be content with what you have; rejoice in the way things are. When you realize there is nothing lacking, the whole world belongs to you. LAO TZU

CHALLENGES ARE GIFTS TOO

We also need to appreciate any difficulties we are going through – because without difficulties, we will not learn. When people are unkind to us, talking nonsense about us and forming unfair judgments, we can either make ourselves depressed and dislike them or we can take it as an opportunity to reflect on what we may have done wrong and how we can improve ourselves. It's often the people who create tremendous difficulties for us who help us to progress on the path by making our journey much more interesting. So rather than being conquered by our own emotions of hatred and unhappiness today, we should take the opportunity to greet those people – to wish them a happy day.

Often, we will join others in complaining about a particular person or group of people because our egos have taken control, allowing our emotions to take over. This is when we need to withdraw from the vicious circle of gossip. If you find yourself in this situation, the best thing to do is to keep your cool and take a step back It's their business, not yours. By practising meditation you will gradually find it increasingly possible to take that step back, to appreciate the good and also the difficult things in life. It's the best tool for taking care of your mind, your happiness.

BE INSPIRED

If the day and the night are such that you greet them with joy, and life emits a fragrance like flowers and sweet-scented herbs, is more elastic, more starry, more immortal – that is your success. All nature is your congratulation, and you have cause momentarily to bless yourself. The greatest gains and values are farthest from being appreciated. We easily come to doubt if they exist. We soon forget them. They are the highest reality. Perhaps the facts most astounding and most real are never communicated by man to man. The true harvest of my daily life is somewhat as intangible and indescribable as the tints of morning or evening. It is a little stardust caught, a segment of the rainbow which I have clutched. HENRY DAVID THOREAU, WALDEN

It is easy for life to become a pattern, or a series of daily habits and to-do lists. The days whizz by, but somehow we feel that we are not quite making the most of them. We know life is precious, but we have many responsibilities; how can we just drop everything to find our inspiration?

And then, suddenly, we get lost – or rather found – in the moment: we read a line of beautiful poetry, we see an old couple holding hands, we cook the most delicious meal or have a breakthrough in our work. We are inspired. These moments are gifts that open us up to happiness.

Our mental and emotional habits keep us chained, and then we experience moments which reveal to us the true spaciousness in our minds and the universe around us. Those moments that, for example, nature offers to us every day through the sunrise and the sunset. A woman I met told me that she'd gone to look at the sunset on the shortest day of the year, the winter solstice, but she wasn't sure if she would be able to see anything because it was a very cloudy day. As she was standing, looking out over a valley in the English countryside, about to turn back for home, the smallest crack appeared in the clouds and the sun rays streamed through. She hadn't expected anything, but walked home with a feeling of potential – such a generous gift from the sun.

When we feel inspired we look beyond and also *into* the mundane and notice what is really important in life, we understand the meaning of life, every day. When inspired we find it so much easier to concentrate, to be in the flow and get things done – we walk with a lightness in our step, we notice the detail, we are happy and that makes others feel happiness too. We feel lucky. Inspiration feeds our inner wisdom and even feeds our body; we are inspired by the food we savour, by human touch, words, even by a walk in nature.

Inspiration leads to action

Somehow, inspiration helps us know what we want to do; and then it's up to us to set our minds to go ahead and do it.

Many people think we Buddhists are only about thinking and never doing, but really it's more that we need to think so that we are then able to do. In other words, if we lack intention, motivation or determination, then we will soon struggle with the 'doing' part of the equation. It's like waking up one morning and immediately trying to go on a diet – you might be surprised or disappointed in yourself when you give up within days or even hours. But if you expected your body to make an instant change without working on your mind first, you were more than likely going to be in for a disappointment.

Appreciation helps you to notice what inspires you and it encourages you to grab that inspiration and turn it into action. So you are no longer following your dreams, always one step behind; instead, you are *being* them, from moment to moment, day to day. You get back to the heart of yourself and what you do.

When you give yourself the space in which to be inspired, you will likely want to share your inspiration, your joy, with others. The happier you feel, the more generous you become. You become a better listener, you reach past your fears of what may or may not happen in your life and open yourself up to the possibilities.

Find your inspiration

Rather than wait for inspiration to find you, why not look for it in your life, in the everyday. I know you'll find it. Be lovable, be kind . . . start there and you'll soon see what inspires you. Appreciation and inspiration are close allies. Just spending a few moments each day reminding yourself of the good in your life gives you a peaceful but powerful energy.

I feel inspired by nature, people, all beings, every day. From the smallest ant to the highest mountain there is always a reason to say 'Wow'. And my job in life is simply to remind people of the good in their hearts and their capacity for love and compassion towards others – to be inspired by this life, so that we may share with others in whatever way we can.

Put simply: inspiration deserves our attention because life deserves our attention. Just as my mother tends her garden, for example, we can all cultivate what inspires us. If we nourish our own talents, then we have so much more to give; then there can be great joy in both our work and play, and we can become more relaxed about ourselves and about others. We can let go of the nonsense that so often rules our day and focus on what really matters. We can let go of the need for praise or blame and even be inspired by our mistakes – as there so often lie the best lessons. We can even be inspired by our fears because breaking through them is often the biggest catalyst for transformation. We can live life daringly.

Be-grateful reminders

- If your mind is looking only for problems, how will you be happy?

- Celebrate all that is good in your life.

- If you ever feel downhearted, think of something you can be grateful for – an instant tonic for the mind.

- Work on your strengths.

- Know that your challenges are gifts too.

- Pay attention to what inspires you.

A Random Act of Happiness

....

Pick a song and dance as though nobody is watching: shake out your tension, let your body do whatever it wants to do and move however you want to move. Do you want to stretch? Do you want to sway or jump up and down? Go with it – dance and laugh and let yourself go.

7

Free Your Mind to Be Happy

The secret of happiness is freedom.
The secret of freedom is courage.
THUCYDIDES

Your mind can be your prison or your mind can set you free; it is mental habits and patterns that so often sabotage your chances for happiness. This chapter considers, therefore, how you might begin to break the ties in your mind and allow thoughts to go more freely, no longer so attached to or weighed down by limiting beliefs that you may have about yourself or others.

BEYOND EGO

Why do you stay in prison when the door is so wide open? RUMI

Before you can begin to loosen the invisible but very strong bounds that are created and then reinforced every day by your mental habits, we need to look a little more closely at the concept of 'ego'. As we saw

99

earlier (see p. 32), the ego is made up of all the beliefs we have built up over time concerning who we think we are and how the world should be. These become so strong over the years that we believe them to be truths. We identify ourselves with our egos because we don't realise there is something deeper and authentic beneath the surface and really the ego exists only in the surface of our minds – it is like a blanket that covers up our inner nature and wisdom.

The ego is a web of stories that begins in childhood: the moment we are given a label – 'naughty' or 'shy' or 'chatty' – the seed of ego is sewn. Gradually, over time, we build up a picture of ourselves and the world around us. And it makes sense that we do this – we are subjective rather than objective beings, after all. But the problems begin to arise because we are so *unaware* of how the ego is really based on perception; it is not the absolute truth that we assume it to be.

The ego is very concerned with 'me' and 'my'; it is very opinionated and likes things to be a certain way for us to then feel secure and happy. But, as we have seen, the ego also very often keeps us trapped in suffering because of its *clinging* nature, either to the things or people we believe *make* us happy today or the things or people we believe we still need, so that we might be happy tomorrow.

Ego is strong, but not very flexible, and so it is quite brittle and easily hurt. Think of the stinging nature of just a single word of criticism or when you feel looked down upon by another person; but then think of how easily your ego falls into the trap of criticising others or making judgments about people according to your own ways of seeing. Attachment to wanting things to be a certain way is very understandable – we all have dreams and desires that we hope will be fulfilled. But it is the grasping nature of the attachment that can be the cause of so much mental suffering.

For example, you might go to work one day, determined to keep in a positive frame of mind and not let your boss or colleagues get to you, whatever challenges may arise. Then, your boss criticises you in front of everyone. You feel a stinging, burning sense of indignation or perhaps shame; you are embarrassed and wonder why you bothered to go to work with good thoughts when there's nothing you can do to stop your boss from humiliating you like this. You feel helpless and wish you could just give up your job, but you're trapped because you need to earn a living to pay for your house and everything else.

There are many emotional and mental habits at play here. Despite your intentions at the beginning of the day, as soon as your boss goes off the script you find yourself reverting to the same old ways of reacting that end up ruining your day. Even your body gets in on the act and teams up with your mind to create that burning sensation. But the good news is that with a bit of practice you can begin to develop the tiniest sense of space around your reactions, so that while you might still feel it was unnecessary for your boss to criticise you in front of everyone, you don't need to cling on to the indignation or embarrassment all day. By developing your awareness, or practising mindful behaviour, you can begin to notice and observe your mental habits, which is the first step towards being able to transform them.

FOLLOWING THE SAME OLD PATTERNS

How do mental habits build up over time? They are the servants of our ego and, in some ways, they appear almost seem to make life easier because we feel we know who we are and how we react to situations; it can be a comfort of sorts to think we know where we stand. Habits allow our minds to become lazy, though, so that negative and painful emotions, like shame or anger or jealousy, rise up without us even noticing and consume our minds in the moment.

Some people cling to mental habits or patterns as a way of discouraging themselves from making changes or taking chances. They take refuge in their habits: 'I'm not the sort of person who likes to travel to new places' or, 'I am always attracted to the wrong type of men'. These are beliefs that we have about ourselves that cover up our confidence, and therefore our happiness.

Limiting self-beliefs

Learn to value yourself, which means: fight for your happiness. AYN RAND

Here are some of the ways in which self-beliefs may present themselves in our minds – the kinds of thoughts that seem to get stuck on replay:

- I can only be happy if I am an extra-good person, all the time.
- I'm never going to be good enough, so I'll just have to grab happiness where I get the chance.
- I must have approval before I can be happy.
- I'm not sure I deserve happiness.
- If I let myself be too happy, I'll be disappointed in the long run.

I can only be happy if I am an extra-good person, all the time

As teachers, we have a phrase that we say to Buddhist practitioners that is 'not to make a big fuss'. We say this to try to help people to relax a little more into their own nature, to know that not one of us is perfect; if we were, then we wouldn't need to walk the path as we'd already have reached enlightenment.

Many people who grew up with very critical parents or who were, perhaps, very good at school and therefore had high expectations placed on them at a young age hold the belief that they have to be extra-special or extra-good to be given permission to be happy. Taking myself as an example – I wasn't very good at studies, but when I was recognised as the reincarnation of the Gyalwang Drukpa, as well as the Indian saint Naropa, I felt an enormous sense of responsibility and worry that I wasn't good enough to look after the Dragon Lineage. These are beliefs that I have encouraged myself to let go of throughout my life; I have learned to trust in myself that I will always do my best. If I spend all my time worrying about whether I am good enough, I will be less helpful to others, as I will be fixated on myself all the time and paralysed by my fear of getting anything wrong.

I'm never going to be good enough,
so I'll just have to grab happiness where
I get the chance

If a person grows up with the belief that they are somehow intrinsically flawed, they might think they don't deserve the deep, peaceful, contented type of happiness and so will grasp instead for sensory, temporary happiness instead. They might spend a great deal of time chasing after this, burning up their money along with their energy. They are frightened of getting to know the real person they are underneath, and if they keep busy enough, they won't have to ever sit still with themselves and do this. If you recognise this type of self-belief, I encourage you to be brave enough (which I know you are) to look into your heart as you read this book and begin to understand the beautiful person within.

I must have approval before I can be happy

As children we soon notice approval – or lack of it – in our parents' eyes. We do cartwheels, blow raspberries and jump into the swimming pool, crying out, 'Look at me, look at me'. And as parents, people make sure to let their children know that they are doing a great job being themselves – growing and developing.

The trouble is that as we get older, we can develop a dependency on the approval of others before we allow ourselves to be happy. So one day we come home from work beaming from ear to ear because our boss said that we were really great at our job; then, the next day, we are upset when they criticise us for making a mistake. If we put our egos up on a pedestal, it can be pretty painful when they inevitably fall off. But if, on the other hand, we can be more accepting of ourselves, taking neither praise nor blame too much to heart, then these things won't hold so much power over our peace of mind.

I'm not sure I deserve happiness

So many people in the world suffer with depression, where all self-worth has drained away, making it hard for them even to get up in the morning. When the mind is in a depression, however great or small, we miss out on life and all its wonders. We struggle in our connections and relationships with others, just when we need their support the most. We lose confidence in our abilities at work or in ourselves as human beings.

A sense of self-worth is an essential ingredient of happiness, but if we only perceive it through our own egos or through material success, then we are really limiting our capacity for happiness. If we develop our minds and, therefore, self-worth as a human being who is connected with others, then we create an amazing foundation of strength on which we can build happiness. It is like the strength of a great tree – with good roots that give us our grounding, but also flexibility and gentleness to be able to bend with the wind.

If I let myself be too happy,
I'll be disappointed in the long run

For some people, expecting the worst is a form of defence which they believe will protect them from experiencing too much pain: if they expect the worst, then they will appreciate the times when the outcome is better than they had imagined. Likewise, if they rock the boat, they might ruin whatever they already have.

I believe in being prepared for the worst – because the only certainty we have in this life is that we will die – but not to live in expectation of bad things happening. If we live this way, our minds spend all the time imagining what might go wrong in the future, rather than what is going right today.

WATCHING OUR MINDS

Awareness, or mindfulness, is an essential practice for helping to break the bonds of our ego – all the myths about ourselves which we believe so deeply to be true, all the prejudices that have built up over time and all the distortions. Mindfulness enables us to begin to understand the difference between pain and suffering; that even when faced with a very painful experience, it is our choice whether we add the suffering of afflictive emotions such as anger, fear or mental anguish to this pain.

It is when we begin to take better notice of how our minds operate that we begin to reconnect with ourselves and, therefore, with our happiness. We start to notice the times when we seem to choose the option of covering up our happiness out of habit, or perhaps because of fear of the unknown. We begin to realise that even though we know we'd like to feel happy for more of the time, we are concerned that if we let ourselves be happy, we'll be setting ourselves up for a fall. And we see how we worry that we don't deserve to be happy, that we might not be a good enough person to feel more than the odd glimpse of joy or that we haven't really earned it.

Then, gradually, we begin to recognise that this is the ego at work: constantly talking and keeping us from reconnecting with our true nature, our fearless, wise, happy nature.

Using just very short periods of meditation and then

developing your sense of mindful awareness during the day, you can begin to choose how you are going to react to challenging situations and people. Many people seem to find themselves dwelling on the negative things that happened during the day or in their life in general. Mindfulness encourages us to notice *all* things that happen, so we begin to acknowledge the good feelings we experienced today, for example, as well as that moment when we felt the sting of a difficult emotion.

Don't be embarrassed to celebrate all the great things in your life; by doing this you will gradually be able to let go of negatives states of mind more easily. They will still come – that is life – but you can allow them to go, rather than attaching too much meaning to them. Mindfulness allows you to see just how changeable your mind is, so that while you might be upset with someone in the moment, you needn't set your mind in stone when it comes to what you think about that person.

If you want to walk around without seeing what is really happening in your life, I am in no position to stop you. It's completely up to you and what you are comfortable with. But if you are curious about the possibility of embracing a different way of seeing, without the usual filters and lenses you look through, then be prepared for more colour and surprises and spontaneity than you could imagine. When you open yourself up to your senses, rather than constantly assuming you think one way or another about a person, a place, a dish of food, anything, you delve into the actual experience.

Spend time with yourself

For some people, it is a good idea to get to know yourself better through experience, while for others, like Jigme Semzang, it is better to do very little so that you may let your inner nature begin to shine through:

The teachings have not only helped me to change mentally, but physically too. A few years ago I was overweight and I walked with a stick. I fell into the habit of either blaming others – for example, causing me stress at work – or blaming myself for not being good enough. I took my health for granted, eating whatever I wanted whenever I wanted it. I was successful at work, earned a very good salary and for many years I was just clinging on to a way of life that I believed gave me my sense of identity. It was as though my business card was my identity. I was always chasing the next promotion, but I was forgetting to take care of myself in the process.

To cut a long story short, I ended up on a Pad Yatra with His Holiness and the nuns from Druk Amitabha. I could hardly make it – I was so unfit and still walking with the stick. But one day His Holiness said to me that if I was slim, I would be strong in my body. That was the moment I began to turn things around and look at things differently. I became healthy and fit, both in my body, and as I began to work on my mind. I stopped running away from myself and went to the retreat in Nepal. I remember asking what prayers or mantras I should do and His Holiness said, 'Nothing. You need to do nothing just for a little while.'

At first it was so hard to just spend all this time with myself, but very slowly I began to understand and my mind began to stop racing. I haven't turned my back on wealth, but I am learning to put it to better use. The biggest lesson I have learned is in any situation to give your best and then leave it. One day I might even stop being such a chatterbox, but that's going to take more practice.

Bees in a jar

Often, when times are challenging, it feels like there isn't much room left for happiness after we've taken account of all the worries, the things we would like to change and the things we don't like so much about our lives. The difficult parts of life seem to take up so much time and space that our minds constantly perpetuate a negative situation or feeling, like a bee trapped in a jar, circling endlessly. We know that somehow we need to change things, but there is no solution in sight and so we feel trapped and tight, with no room to breathe, let alone feel the warmth of happiness.

One of the greatest benefits of meditation is to create a bit of space in your mind. It won't offer you instant solutions to your problems, but it will help to reveal where you have become caught up in negative thoughts that end up consuming the mind:

1. Sit for a few moments and bring your focus back to your breath (see p. 54).
2. Now imagine your thoughts as bees in a jar, buzzing around, bumping up against each other and the sides with nowhere to go. What's on your mind?
3. Now unscrew the lid and open up the jar, allowing the bees, and therefore your thoughts, to go free as if in a meadow, about their business. See the blue sky; feel the warmth of the sun.
4. Your thoughts and emotions will come and go – they just have a little more space now.

FREE YOUR MIND FROM THE USUAL LABELS

When we aren't paying attention, we cling to so many things with our minds that we tie ourselves up in knots, unable to move or think freely.

I always think, for example, about how attached people in different countries are to their labels of measurement: 'But what is that exactly in miles?' or, 'I can't understand you – can you tell me in pounds and ounces?' Similarly, we break up time into things that we can measure – seconds, hours, days, years – but meanwhile, time just goes on its own way, completely regardless of how we might label it. And just like happiness, we will never pin it down.

When it comes to labelling ourselves and other people, and then strongly believing in those labels, we create the possibility for tension and disagreements, both within ourselves and with others; there is a lack of harmony. Remember all those limiting beliefs we talked about earlier – for example, believing that we have to be perfect before we can be happy? Not only do we set ourselves up for a fall with such thoughts, we tend to see faults in others that either consciously or subconsciously we fear are what is wrong with us too. If we are highly critical of ourselves, we will tend to be highly critical of others. We might convince ourselves that we have a highly developed sense of justice or of what is fair, but when looked at from an alternative angle this might be perceived as being highly judgmental and demanding of others. It's the same behaviour, just a different label.

Breaking the illusion

As we develop our awareness that we all create labels based on our own perceptions and experiences, we realise that we don't need to cling to any of them or take up such a defensive stance when somebody's opinion is different from ours. So it's ok if my friend is perfect to me, but not perfect to you. Why should we get angry at each other? Let's respect our differences and understand that there is no need to hold on so tightly to our beliefs that we never have the flexibility to bend with the wind. And then let's have a cup of tea and talk about something happy.

When we begin to understand this, we see that differences don't matter. We set ourselves free from what is 'mine' and what is 'yours'. These are the kinds of tools that may be used to cut yourself free; to cut the bonds of your ego and set your mind free.

No fixed concept

It is very good to hear from people like Lee who are putting things into practice from the teachings and seeing how they work for them – or not – in the hustle and bustle of real life:

After attending a retreat in Hong Kong almost seven years ago, I can still remember very clearly His Holiness's teaching on 'no fixed concept' resonating in my mind whenever I am stuck with a problem: that if we let ourselves, we may always have the ability to look at a problem from a better angle. I find this teaching very powerful as we have so many fixed concepts of ourselves, and society also imposes many concepts on each and every one of us. This has brought about a great transformation for myself as the fixed concept of self creates a lot of obstacles of 'me and mine' in our daily lives and brings pain and suffering not just to ourselves, but also to our loved ones.

In the workplace, we also have many fixed concepts of how things should be executed, but have no time to spend listening to our colleagues and opening our hearts and minds to embrace others into our lives. If we have no concept of ourselves, we are always open to comments and we will be able to transform comments to something positive. We will be able to check ourselves and learn something positive from every situation. When we are joyfully working on a project, we will naturally project positive energy and attract like-minded people to us. This brings about not only great joy in working, but also positive energy to the entire atmosphere and we will be able to execute anything effortlessly as the mind is light, relaxed and joyful and will be an inspiration for others too! This brings about the concept of 'we' and not 'I'!

Whenever I am stuck in a situation, I am reminded of 'living in the moment', as we are always projecting our minds forward, worrying unnecessarily about everything and anything that comes into our minds and missing the moment and getting angry and frustrated. I take a breather and check whether I am practising 'no fixed concept' and then I will feel rejuvenated and continue working joyfully moment by moment.

WITH A FREE MIND WE CAN EXPERIENCE AUTHENTIC HAPPINESS

Authentic happiness should be experienced right now. Sometimes, we come across temporary happiness – a piece of cake might give you this type of sensory, pleasure-based happiness or completing a race, giving a speech, passing a test . . . Happiness is definitely there, but it is short-term. It is a surface type of happiness; it is something that comes, but then burns out quickly.

We need to begin to understand our own minds – our motivations, wants and needs. For example, we might contemplate why have we become such voracious consumers? Why do we go out constantly and buy new things that we don't need but have a craving for? It is a distraction, a sticking plaster that keeps our minds occupied. Of course, there is the temporary feeling of light relief, of giving ourselves a bit of a treat or improving our comfort, but the trouble is that when we try to find comfort or relief through 'things' we tend to end up needing more of them just to sustain the feeling. We have wardrobes full of clothes we hardly ever wear, we throw away food uneaten. Sometimes it feels as though we have replaced 'people' with 'things'.

There is nothing wrong at all with wanting to have nice things, to look smart or attractive. But when we attach emotions to these possessions or somehow identify ourselves with the things we have we are more

115

likely to feed dissatisfaction rather than happiness. We get caught up in the cycle of striving for more when perhaps we might even benefit from less.

You will no doubt have heard this many times, but no person ever cared very much about their possessions once they were on their deathbed. So as you begin to reflect on how your life is shaping up and what you would like to prioritise in the precious time you have, consider how attached you are to being a consumer and whether it brings you the same kind of happiness as the loving relationships in your life or being fulfilled by what you do.

Authentic happiness is deep and lasting, it is always there, but we just don't see it. It is easy to perceive this type of happiness as something we may experience in the future, but that right now we aren't ready for it. Don't think that you have to walk miles and miles down the road to find this happiness; you can experience it right now. Many people misunderstand this and believe there must be a very difficult journey, and then when you reach your destination you will be happy. Why not enjoy the journey, why not be happy with every step? This is your chance to be happy, from this moment every day and every minute of your life.

Free-your-mind-to-be-happy Reminders

- Your ego places conditions on your happiness, telling you what you still need to be happy or what you can't lose if you want to stay happy.

- Authentic happiness is unconditional.

- Get to know your beliefs and how they either help or hinder you. Awareness and attention are the first steps to making your mind your friend.

- Begin to observe your perceptions and practise seeing them as fluid, rather than fixed; be open to new ideas and points of view and be willing to see things differently.

- When you are upset by a situation or person, ask yourself 'Am I going to attach myself to this?' You don't need to let a fleeting emotion ruin your day.

A Random Act of Happiness

....

Every time you buy a new piece of clothing: pick a piece from your cupboard and take it to the charity shop in exchange. We don't need to be so attached to all our things so that they overflow, let them come and go and make someone else happy in the process.

8

Change Your Mental Habits

The essence of the beautiful is unity in variety.
W. SOMERSET MAUGHAM

We can't often change the physical reality of a given situation, but our minds have quite an amazing effect on how we perceive, interpret and therefore cope with it. In Buddhism, we talk about the 'dualistic' mind, which basically describes how the human mind tends to try and see everything in black and white, good or bad, while knowing that life rarely fits into such neat boxes. Even when we have a conversation, we often feel like we are on one side or the other – that we have to take a stance or a point of view and defend it with all our intellect and verbal skills, ideally so the other person will back down and we will 'win'. But lucky is the person who sees every conversation as a chance to learn and see something in life from another person's perspective.

Kashyapa, consider the world of three thousand great thousand worlds and the grasses, trees, forests, as

119

well as the medicinal herbs, in their many varieties, with their different names and colors which the mountains, streams, valleys and flatlands produce. A thick cloud spreads out, covering the three thousand great thousand worlds, raining on them equally everywhere at the same time, its moisture reaching every part. The grasses, trees, forests and medicinal herbs – those of small roots, small stalks, small branches and small leaves, those of medium-sized roots, medium-sized stalks, medium-sized branches, medium-sized leaves or those of large roots, large stalks, large branches, and large leaves, and also all the trees, whether great or small, according to their size, small, medium, or large – all receive a portion of it. From the rain of the one cloud each according to its nature grows, blossoms, and bears fruit. Although they grow from the same ground and are moistened by the same rain, still, all the grasses and trees are different.

THE LOTUS SUTRA

Just as all the herbs and flowers and trees in the *Lotus Sutra* have unique potential, even though they all receive the rain from one cloud, so is true for us human beings. We each see things from our own unique perspective, made up of our experiences, our personalities and emotions. All of these different ways of seeing are interesting and valid, and so if we can encourage ourselves to look at situations from alternative angles, we might dissolve some of the blocks between us and our happiness.

Life is full of surprises. Why would we use the phrase, 'every cloud has a silver lining' if it were as simple as saying one thing is good or another is bad?

Same experience, different experience

Life rarely goes perfectly according to our plans; it's up to us whether we see that as a problem or a blessing, as Cathy discovered while on retreat with us at Druk Amitabha Mountain:

When we go on retreat to the nunnery at Druk Amitabha Mountain, we walk down the steep hill to the famous Swayambhunath Stupa in Kathmandu for kora or circumambulation, which means walking around the circumference of the stupa a certain number of times before giving an offering. This time we went in the evening and so made an offering of lights by lighting as many candles as possible to send out good wishes to the world.

His Holiness always walks at an incredible pace and I always try to stay with the front group. I was running to keep up when I managed to trip where the side of the road falls away into the gutter and twisted my ankle quite badly, so that I could only walk very slowly and gingerly around the stupa.

I soon fell way behind the main group at the front. This was new for me; I had been forced to slow down by an unfortunate occurrence, but it turned out to be a wonderful and new experience. As I walked I noticed so much more along the way. Life around the Swayambhunath Stupa is there in all its colours. It is a very raw place where the most unfortunate people will go to die, spending their last days under a sheet of plastic if they are lucky and then finally laid to rest under a white sheet, with the charity of strangers paying for the funeral cremation. It is also a place of constant activity, a whirl of colour, community, commerce and gathering.

As I reached the place where we would make the offering of lights there were already some nuns there, quietly lighting dozens upon dozens of thin white candles up the steps of the stupa. It was so peaceful and beautiful. I knelt down and began to light candles, enjoying the quiet company and taking in the energy of the place while thinking about the offering.

By slowing down, I was able to see the same experience with new eyes. It was a good lesson for me, both to not always push to be at the front, which I must admit I do as much in life as I do during the kora, and also to be open to seeing things from different perspectives. I hope I will be able to apply that lesson, whether it is in being more relaxed about differences of opinion or that it's ok if things don't go according to plan – it might end up being very interesting!

THE MIND IS LIMITLESS

Through his advanced mind training and meditation, the Buddha was known to go through walls, through solid rock and even fly across mountain tops. Of course, this defies our usual logic and the laws of physics. But, through the power of his unlimited mind, Buddha was able to go beyond accepted conventions, beyond all labels and understand that what we see as a wall is a perception and so might easily be walked through.

Perhaps an easier example to think about is water: for fish, water is home, but while we humans might be given life by drinking it, water would kill us before it could be our home. So the meaning or purpose of water changes depending on the angle from which we are looking at it. In other words, we don't need to cling to any one definition. The same is true of happiness: we don't need to try and define it – it can mean different things to different people. As the Zen saying goes: 'To her lover a beautiful woman is a delight; to a monk she is a distraction; to a mosquito, a good meal.'

Many years ago when white people first arrived in Tibet, the people there were very scared of them because they looked so strange with their yellow hair and blue eyes – they had never seen people like this before. They would clap at the white people, as was their custom to shoo something scary away; but the white people, for their part, felt very happy when they were clapped, as in their culture it was a sign of appreciation.

As you begin to make more of a conscious choice to step outside of your usual mental habits, you will naturally learn to see things differently, as you will no longer be so firmly rooted in your usual position – or at least you will notice that you are looking at the world through your own individual set of filters. Why would this help when it comes to nourishing happiness as your state of mind? As you can imagine, if we always look at things from the same angle, we begin to set very fixed ideas of what we believe to be right or good; we get into a mental rut, rather than allowing our state of mind to flow and be flexible. We even begin to set our definition of happiness into stone: if the picture of our lives looks a certain way, it's ok and we can be happy; but if anything changes in that picture, we resist and feel anxious that we will no longer be happy. When we only allow ourselves one way of seeing we are easily angered or irritated when other people don't fit in with our opinion of what is appropriate behaviour; we have a long list of 'shoulds' and 'shouldn'ts' that make us highly critical and judgmental.

If we can't develop the ability to step into another person's shoes, then it is very difficult to make meaningful connections or have empathy and compassion for others. We can become quite isolated in our own minds, unable to bend or adapt – which is why giving our minds a bit of a workout every now and then is a very good idea. Just like a car engine, if we leave the mind alone for too long, it becomes rusty and what should be moving parts become stiff or stuck.

SEE THINGS DIFFERENTLY

If you develop the ability to see things differently sometimes, then your idea of happiness will be flexible. Perhaps you have always seen the glass as half empty; now is your chance to choose to look from another angle and see it as half full.

Take money as an example. Whether people have a great deal of money or not very much at all, there will still be different ways of seeing it. I know men and women who have become very successful through their work. Some feel very comfortable with this, they truly appreciate the fruits of their labour and are not terribly attached to material things; they are very happy that they are able to give a great deal away while also having a nice roof over their head and providing a good education for their children. But I also meet people who have so much one might think they could never have any worries about money, yet who, from their own point of view, worry constantly about losing their riches or feel jealous of a neighbour whose house or car is even bigger than theirs. They live in fear that it will all disappear, even to the point of being miserly. I feel sorrow for these people who put off their happiness because of a way of seeing. When I connect with people who are very fixed or solid in their views like this, my hope is that gradually, with practice, the ropes that hold their minds down will loosen and dissolve. Then they will understand the great good they might do with their success, and how they might accept that it's ok for them to enjoy themselves too.

I have visited many holy cave retreats and monasteries where masters practised and attained enlightenment. Visiting these holy places gives us great encouragement, but when I see ruined buildings and statues, I feel quite sad and ask why would humans destroy beautiful things? I know it is because they are holy places, and that very sadly some people of different religions will fight over their beliefs and end up destroying places of prayer. I wish for people to forget about them being holy, at least try to appreciate the beauty. It is the same if we have a mind that is limited and only able to accept our own ideas of right and wrong, we would become like those people who destroy beautiful things in others' cultures, traditions and countries, we would become those unhappy ones living in a box. When things do not follow our way, they have to be destroyed. This is the same as relationships, when our friends or family do not follow our instructions, we have the tendency to be angry and mad at them, though never at ourselves.

This is why I always say, watch your mind, if you can guard your mind, your speech and actions would be okay. Most of the time, we don't do that. Instead, we are always looking outward, measuring others against our own peculiar standards. Do not expect others to follow our ways, each of us has our own path, some may be similar, but never exactly the same.

Our minds create our world

It is a joy for me to see how the experience of our Pad Yatras may bring moments of true understanding to volunteers, like Joanna, who then take these moments into their lives:

One of the most inspiring experiences I have had is a quiet joyfulness just in the middle of turbulent emotional and strong physical challenges during the Pad Yatras. What I appreciate mostly is the inner space which opens spontaneously within, while strong emotions arise, dissolve, arise and dissolve . . . and still joyfulness radiates from within. Like a lotus in the middle of mud.

I will never forget the taste of a piece of old bread which I first refused to take, but soon took the decision: this is our dinner. Then I stopped wanting something else and the old bread became delicious and yummy. Later I realised it is how the mind creates realities. Often, since then, similar experiences have happened in my daily life and the piece of old bread reminds me how to change my mind and be satisfied with what is there now.

Growing awareness of my own behavioural patterns helps me to offer a better support to my clients. This simple understanding and acceptance towards myself goes automatically to my closest relationships, to my clients and to others. I listen better, think more clearly and take care with my words. The changes I have experienced within myself keep giving me a deeper confidence in everyone's abilities to change towards wellbeing and to meet without fear the challenges of life.

Pause to reflect

If you were to look into a still pond at night and see the reflection of the moon, it would look exactly the same as if you were looking directly at the moon itself. To our eyes there is no difference and yet we know that the moon in the lake is just a reflection, an illusion.

You can use your own mirror for this exercise: simply take a minute to look at yourself in the mirror. You can see every little detail – how tall you are, how many grey hairs you have today. But despite appearances, it is not real. Like the moon in the lake, the face you see is just a reflection.

This is a contemplative meditation that helps us to understand that nothing in the world has a fixed reality. It improves our ability to understand how it is our minds that give meaning to everything around us – that there is no one truth, but only perception and appearance. This explains why two people who have experienced exactly the same situation might have very different perceptions of it. As a simple example, think of when you are on holiday in the countryside – when it rains you are very disappointed, but the farmers are rejoicing. So is rain good or bad? There is no fixed answer.

The aim of such contemplation is to train our minds, so that we are able to step into another person's shoes to try and see things from their point of view, even when we are initially angered or upset by their actions. It's so easy to judge others, and we often forget to pause and see that usually there are many conditions involved in a given situation and that we might not be perfect ourselves. After all, if we were perfect, we would be Buddha, and Buddha wouldn't have had an argument in the first place!

It's up to us: we always have a choice whether to cling on to one narrow view of the world or open our minds up to embracing difference and seeing the beauty in variety.

The illusion of reality

It can be difficult to consider that our concept of reality is just that – a concept, rather than a universal truth. How can we have anything concrete to show for our lives if reality is just an illusion of the mind? Trevor is a lawyer, which can be a very adversarial role – on one side of the 'truth' or another:

The Gyalwang Drupka frequently says that we need to cultivate a view that the world around us is like a dream or an illusion. Frankly, it had scared me to put his words into practice because it felt as though I would lose touch with reality. Recently, I have tried following his teaching, and it has had the opposite effect. I feel more grounded and open to possibility.

Like many people, my world is frequently governed by anxiety, anger or fear. I work as a lawyer and constantly feel scrutinised by opposing counsel or even my colleagues. It is the nature of a profession – that in the United States at least – is deliberately designed to be adversarial. This sense of scrutiny leads to a pervasive sense of insecurity that causes me to feel anxious or angry a lot of the time.

By attempting to cultivate a view that the world is dream-like, the anxiety and anger have begun to dissipate. I believe that these feelings were the result of me tightly grasping to my expectations, my views and even my own sense of self. Seeing these things as a dream gives me space. I do not need to worry so much if the reality in which I live is not substantial.

Seeing the illusion-like nature of our reality is not a sojourn into nihilism. To the contrary: viewing reality as dream-like has allowed me to let go of negative emotions and act with more compassion. When I hear nasty, unfounded words from opposing counsel, I grow less angry because these words – and the emotions to which they give rise – hold a less concrete meaning. Likewise, if I need to confront someone with whom I am working over a difficult issue, I am better able to do so without anger. I can take the time to focus on what the other person needs because I have the space to see my views as no more or less important than theirs.

Rather than losing touch with reality, I have gained a better grasp of it. I am given space and openness to see vast, dreamy possibilities – including the possibility of acting with love to others, even in my own most difficult moments.

If you are brave and look at yourself openly and honestly, willing to learn from your experiences, to change yourself and develop your life for the better, then you will certainly feel vulnerable and you might even be a little fearful of what you might see. But if you have the courage to look at your own imperfections, quirks and things that you would like to improve, then you will also be understanding of the imperfections and vulnerabilities of others. Rather than being quick to judge or criticise, you will have more patience because you will know we are all in the same boat, doing our best to be happy. You will be more accepting of difference, which makes for a much easier, happier way of life.

Change-your-mental-habits reminders

- See the beauty in difference.

- Remember that every cloud has a silver lining, if you are willing to see it.

- If you disagree with someone, make a conscious effort to step into their shoes and see the situation from their point of view. Even if you continue to disagree, you will gain some understanding.

- It is your mind that creates your world, so if you ever don't like what you see, have the courage to look into your mind and make a change.

A Random Act of Happiness

Bake bread: a loaf of bread brings us
back to the simple essence of life, plus the
pure pleasure of seeing, smelling and tasting
the fruit of our efforts. When we remind
ourselves where our food comes from (like
pulling a carrot out of the earth in the morning
and cooking it for our supper that night) bread
shows us something about sustenance and also
potential: who would think such a wonderful
thing could come from flour and water
and yeast?

9

Embrace Your Fears

*Happy is the man who has broken the chains
which hurt the mind, and has given up worrying
once and for all.*

OVID

We have so much to feel good about, yet we spend
all our time worrying about the things that aren't quite
right, that might go wrong or that we might lose. It is
the 'not knowing' that sends our minds into a tailspin
– playing out possible scenarios and how we might
react to them and wishing we could just know the
outcome, rather than be faced with so much chance
and uncertainty in life. We try to forge a path of
certainty: if we don't take any risks, then maybe we'll
be ok and not have to face anything too difficult.

But it is often in our attempts to safeguard our
happiness that we instead stifle it and become increasingly fearful or anxious. And if we do not look after
our minds, then uncertainty can easily become associated with and attached to fear: fear of the great
unknown, fear of death and even fear of life. Worrying

is a mental drain; believing instead that anything is possible requires the same investment of energy, only channelled differently. You put your energy to good use, rather than letting it burn away for nothing.

The teachings have taught me to trust myself and to be confident, to be fearless. You need to be a little bit brave to look your idiosyncrasies in the eye and work on yourself; to develop your life and get closer to your nature. Looking in the mirror like this can be a painful process but as His Holiness said to me once, if you don't cut now, when? So in the past years I have been cutting the ties created by my mind – all the fears and worries about who I am and how my life is turning out.

JIGME SEMZANG

FREE YOURSELF FROM FEAR AND ANXIETY

Happy is the man who has given up worrying. Attaching yourself to your worries limits you and robs your mind of the mental freedom that allows you to be happy. It's a perpetual circle of the same kinds of thoughts feeding off each other and going around and around. They take up precious time and they stifle happiness, keeping it suffocated and invisible beneath the surface of a tense, stressed-out mind. Even small, daily worries can build up over time, leaving little room for other things. Then you feel small and inhibited, your thoughts become small and inhibited and, as a result, the same thing happens to your words and actions. So you feel limited in your potential, meaning that you are restricting yourself by allowing worries to take centre stage all the time in your mind.

If you are someone who tends towards worrying, and you certainly won't be alone if you are, then if you begin to practise even a few minutes of meditation, focusing on the breath (see p. 54) and releasing thoughts as you breathe out, your mind will begin to feel more calm and spacious. Instead of holding on to worries and constantly turning them over and over, wearing out your mind, you will begin to acknowledge them for what they are and allow them to dissolve or float away.

Focus on happiness

If you could take a picture each day of your happiness, what would it look like? One day it might be a familiar face, another day something completely surprising and new. It might be a challenge or fear that you embraced and stepped through. It might be a connection you made. Every day is a chance for happiness. If you take one small action each day towards your happiness, in time those small actions will change the bigger picture and transform your life.

WHERE THERE IS FEAR THERE IS HOPE

I meet many people who feel they could do so much more if they could just throw out their fears and anxieties. But rather than try to ignore fears, perhaps there is something to be said for looking into the heart of them, accepting them and then walking through them. If you can look at your fears or worries from another angle, you will often find something inspiring, something you truly want to do with your life. Someone who is afraid to get married, for example, also knows deep down the potential for happiness in being in a loving, committed relationship. In exactly the same place we imagine failure there is success. There should be no shame or regret when we turn away from our fears and walk away, but equally, why not jump in and use them as our inspiration? They hold great potential for growth.

Nowhere to hide

Kate does not practise Buddhism, but comes to the retreats for the philosophical teachings, to explore ideas:

I have been to Druk Amitabha Mountain three times on retreat, and each time I am confronted with the realisation that there is nowhere to hide there, physically, mentally or emotionally. The image I have of myself comes right up to the surface and then crumbles away as I quickly realise I am not special, but at the same time we are all as special and important as each other. I arrive with the labels, 'I am not a Buddhist', 'I am shy' and 'I am not a group person'. And then I realise that to the nuns I am simply a guest who is staying with them for a few days, no labels required. I remember one morning I received some bad news over the phone and I came out of the dorm room crying. As I was passing a nun, she touched my face and said, 'Don't be afraid'. It's funny, with English not being her first language she made me realise just how much I can let fear and anxiety get in the way of my happiness. But I can also be quite good at letting go and jumping in, giving things a go. That's how I ended up at this incredible place at the foot of the Himalayas in the first place, the place that reminds me to let go of the fussiness, be myself without the need for labels and keep jumping in.

Why not?

I love this question. It makes my mind happy!

It is understandable that people often fall into the trap of trying to come up with excuses why they shouldn't do what is their heart's desire – why they should let some kind of fear or anxiety put them off. But these two little words – why not? – help to dissolve the monsters and propel us forward. Why not give it a go? Why not take that chance? Why not make a leap? Many very famous and successful business people in the world tell stories, with big smiles on their faces, of all the times they tried and failed at things. We might wonder how they can be so happy about their failures, but not one of them ever felt sad about giving something a try, even if it didn't always work out. It seems that even bumps along the path can be a source of happiness in some ways.

I'm not saying we need to take risks to be happy, but rather that we should be less controlled by the limiting thoughts that prevent us from giving things a try. Doubts will give our minds the impression they are there to protect us, but it is when we allow ourselves to be vulnerable that sometimes we do the most amazing things with our lives. We might fall in love, or accomplish something we never thought possible. We stretch the boundaries of our minds, creating new space to grow.

DEVELOP YOUR LIFE

If you are somehow fearful of doing what you really want to do in life because you feel you lack the back-up of support or somebody to rely on in case things go wrong, then this is the perfect time to develop yourself. You are overlooking the one person who you can lean on, who gives you strength and courage. That person is you.

Many people have lost confidence in themselves. They worry that if they make a big mistake, no one will be there to pick them up, so it is better to play it safe and avoid risks as much as possible. This is a very understandable position, but it relies on the fabrication or self-delusion that if we don't change, the world around us will remain the same too – our job will be secure, our house will be safe and so on. And yet industries are changing all the time; the world economy almost completely collapsed just a few years ago.

Nothing is certain; nothing stays the same for ever. So when you look into your heart, beneath the worries and the fears and the uncertainties, and see the confident you who feels inspired by something or wants to take a new direction, allow yourself to start connecting and interacting with that inner confidence. You will see that life is too short to waste so much time working through the fifty possible scenarios that may result from one decision or choice. Why don't you see for yourself what is going to happen and really experience the richness of your life?

Putting positive thoughts into action

Ask yourself: if you could make the world a happier place today, and you couldn't fail, what would you do? You may want to contemplate this question or even write down your thoughts – whatever works for you. Consider what really motivates you. For me, I always feel 'activated' when I consider what we might be able to do when it comes to being more friendly with the environment and with nature. We have turned these thoughts into focused action by collecting all of our rubbish for recycling, putting up solar panels and asking guests to be mindful of their water usage when they visit our monasteries.

So today, I invite you to turn your own positive thoughts into positive words and actions, deepen your connections and interactions with the world around you and share all the wonderful love and kindness that you have in your heart.

FEELING THE FEAR

Men come and they go and they trot and they dance, and never a word about death. All well and good. Yet when death does come – to them, their wives, their children, their friends – catching them unawares and unprepared, then what storms of passion over-whelm them, what cries, what fury, what despair! . . . let us deprive death of its strangeness, let us frequent it, let us get used to it . . . To practice death is to practice freedom. MONTAIGNE

141

We contemplate the 'Five Remembrances' (below) to help release ourselves from fear. These are designed to remind us of the changing nature of life, and when we reflect on that we become less clinging to our self-beliefs and our fears of what might – or might not – happen. If we are afraid to let go because we have been let down or hurt in the past, or if our past mistakes still loom large in our imaginations, we need to remind ourselves to live in the present, to appreciate everything good in our lives today, to know that we are going to do our best today and not live under the dark cloud of expectation.

1. There is no way to escape growing old.
2. There is no way to escape ill health at some point during life.
3. There is no way to escape death.
4. Everything and everyone that I love is subject to the nature of change. There is no way to escape being separated from them.
5. The only things that I own are my thoughts, my words and my actions. There is no escape from the consequences of these; they are the ground upon which I stand.

Contemplating these statements gently allows us to bring our fears right into our consciousness. Rather than deny them, we put them into a context that reminds us they are really the same as everyone else's. We cannot stop time, every second we are getting older, we will experience ill health at some point in life (although, of course, there is much we can do to promote good health), and eventually we will die. Once we genuinely accept these things we awaken to our lives as they exist right now: we rejoice in our relationships, rather than looking for the cracks; we make the most of our body and health, doing everything we can to take care of ourselves; we accept past hurts and mistakes, but no longer allow them to influence our present or our future.

The remembrances are raw and honest, and because of that they cut through the usual layers of excuses and justifications for not facing our fears – for maintaining the status quo of life, rather than rocking the boat. As you are honest, your inner nature will come to the surface, so that you may begin to feel even more comfortable in your own skin and more fearless in how you approach your life. You will hear what is in your heart and have the courage to follow what you are telling yourself.

The realisation that the only way to change your life is by changing your own thoughts and actions, frees you to focus on what you can improve, rather than holding on to mistakes or hurts that have been and gone. Today is what really counts – come back to your present and you will come into the richness of your life.

Time waits for no man, so don't put off your own happiness for another minute.

Embrace-your-fears reminders

- You can never be certain of the future, so make the commitment today to stop spending so much time and mental energy worrying about it.

- Be inspired by your fears – they often hold the greatest potential for your growth.

- Ask yourself, 'Why not?' Why not take that chance? Why not give it a go?

- If you feel afraid but want to step out of your comfort zone to try something new and exciting, practise focusing on the breath (see p. 54) and as your body and mind relax, ask the question: 'What do I really want?' Never be afraid to listen to your heart.

- As you begin to connect with your inner nature and inner voice through meditation and mindfulness, your confidence will grow.

A Random Act of Happiness

....

Think of three strengths that you have: for example, are you kind, creative, good with detail, a good negotiator, adaptable, optimistic or a strong leader? How can you put those three strengths to use today to benefit others in some way?

10

Be Friendly with All Your Emotions

For every minute you are angry, you lose sixty seconds of happiness.

RALPH WALDO EMERSON

Negative emotions such as anger, greed and pride are corrosive to one's balanced and happy state of mind, but rather than try to suppress or ignore them, it is better to become more aware of when they come and where they come from. By acknowledging negative emotions and understanding why you are experiencing them, it will be easier to let them go.

One of the greatest obstacles to happiness that I see increasingly often is anger. This saddens me so much. There is the obvious, extremely dangerous anger that creates the mind of a terrorist or someone who harms another person. And then there is the anger that I see on the streets on a regular basis. People today seem to become angry with hardly any provocation – you can feel it bubbling up even as they sit there. Or you might see somebody walking in front of another person and you will feel the anger of that first person flare up immediately, like a lit match. So someone walked in front of them . . . so what? Is it a big deal?

It can sometimes seem as though the accepted norms of a society's behaviour feed this type of anger; the rules are giving people the sense that it is their right to be angry. I met a woman from England who told me that there are 'silent' carriages on the trains there; this is a nice idea in principle, but when people don't see the signs and are chatting on the phone, others around them will begin to simmer and then boil over in their rage, throwing the culprit disapproving glares and pointing at the signs. Of course, I understand that we are all trying to act according to a good set of ethics, but we have become too quick to get upset when other people don't know the rules or have a different set of ideas altogether. I must admit I can be quite a chatterbox and so I'm sure I would get told off on one of these trains – but it is the anger in the reaction that worries me; all it does is cause suffering, and mainly to the person who is holding on to it.

Without 'friendliness' happiness cannot be there in our minds. If we are not friendly towards others, towards nature or towards ourselves, then we don't give happiness a chance. So even when you are taking a very honest look at yourself in the mirror and you don't like what you see at first, be gentle with yourself and always be friendly with all your emotions. If you can't be compassionate to yourself, then how can you help to make the world a happier place? You are wasting all of your amazing potential by concentrating on feeling bad about the things you don't like about yourself and others.

You don't need to carry your anger with you

Carrie's passion is her strength, but occasionally we all need to recognise when our emotions are holding us back. They are still very important, but we may develop the confidence to acknowledge them and then let them go, rather than carry them all with us:

I remember being on a Pad Yatra when we came across a man who it turned out was buying historic artifacts at very cheap prices from the local villages with the intention to make a big profit once he got back to his home country. As a lawyer, I was incensed by this man and I became very angry with him, right there, on the mountain path. I felt I had to stand up for the people and their villages, some of which we would be visiting along the way of the Pad Yatra. The argument became so heated that we almost came to blows, which is crazy because this man could have literally pushed me off the side of the mountain. Fortunately, no one was hurt, but I was still so angry and when I spoke to His Holiness later that day I told him all about it and how we must make sure the man is arrested and prosecuted. His Holiness told me, yes, yes, we will make sure to let the authorities know so that they could decide what to do, but then he looked straight at me and laughed that wonderful, kind laugh of his. I was still so full of anger I couldn't believe His Holiness was laughing at me, but then I realised what a comical scene we must've made: two people shouting at each other on the side of a mountain in the Himalayas. He then said to me, 'Now, are you going to leave your anger here, or carry it with you every day, because we still have a long way to go.'

It's amazing that when you look directly at your anger or craving, for example, it often evaporates there and then. And while it is very difficult to do this in the heat of the moment, if you give yourself a chance to investigate when you are feeling calmer, then it often becomes a way in itself to get out of negative thinking and see things a little differently.

Pause to reflect

Allow yourself the space to learn from interactions, to learn from your friends, for example, or from your disappointments and even your anger. By being a better watcher of your mind, and therefore your reactions, you will gradually give yourself that little bit of space which will take some of the heat out of the situation. If you don't give yourself space, then rather than learn from these things you might feel as though everything is going down in a negative way. And tomorrow, instead of feeling happiness or feeling motivated to make a change in your life or to develop and take care of your mind, you will feel like you have a hangover in your mind and your heart. It is as though a heaviness takes over, which can be the cause of a great deal of unnecessary suffering, and rather than picking yourself up to find out what interesting things today has in store, you remain stuck in negativity.

Our emotions are our teachers and usually signal when we need to interact more, rather than continue to hold back and feel jealous or frustrated or fearful of what might happen. So when you get upset with people, don't run away or let yourself get carried away by emotions like anger or disappointment. Just give yourself a second and allow the space to come between you and the anger. Realise that the sensation of anger in your body is just that, a fleeting sensation just like a cloud momentarily covering up the sun's warmth. Allow it to pass, instead of holding on to it. Understand that you are not anger, you are experiencing anger. Then you will receive one of the biggest lessons of all.

For many of you there is no space at all right now between you and your emotions. Anger or impatience feel as though they are instantaneous, as though you have no control over them. It will take a great deal of conscious effort, but if you can allow even the smallest gap between a thought you have in your mind and the emotions that rush in, you will begin to let the river of your mind flow just a little more smoothly around the rocks and over the rapids – not because you are blindly drifting along, buffeted by the waves, but because you are becoming a great navigator, aware of what is going around you. You will begin to notice that you feel more prepared to be friendly with your emotions, that you feel you have more time to gently meet and flow around the obstacles in your life, rather than lurching from one extreme reaction to the other. By doing so, you get to enjoy the journey so much more: you have the time to look around and notice all the beauty, and you have the chance to listen, whether to the birds or to the people who are dear to you in your life, rather than everything being drowned out by your waterfall of thoughts and emotions.

Of course, you still have all these emotions, but by putting a little space around them, you may get to know them better and understand where they come from. The best time to practise is when you feel an emotion like anger or impatience: you need not see your emotions as enemies, which will make you feel even more upset as you feel bad about being an angry or impatient person, but you can turn things on their head and instead use them as friends. Instead of rejecting the emotions, think about how you might transform them. It is like fighting with someone who is much stronger than you: the best way is to talk with them – and the same goes for your emotions. Investigate them, ask yourself what is their purpose and remind yourself that whatever happens in the moment, you don't then need to cling to your reactions.

If you hold on to anger, you will end up burning yourself. When you feel so sure about your own definitions of what is right and what is wrong, you chase your own happiness away through stubbornness and ego clinging. You replay arguments or situations in your head, and rather than making peace, you feel even more outrage or hurt as you re-experience a situation over and over again. Anger and other negative emotions have a way of closing up the mind, making everything feel very tight, as though you can't breathe. A mind filled with hate destroys all good things and eats away at your capacity for compassion and kindness. It is impossible to feel joy if you are consumed by anger.

I say to people, 'Sit on your cushion to look at your emotions.' When we remove all the other distractions of life, we are left just with our minds. Then we can use what is in our minds to practise patience, compassion and love and emotions like anger and jealousy begin to dissolve into emptiness. I like the phrase 'all things being equal'. Because at the end of the day, all things *are* equal – nothing is permanent, everything fades, so why cling on so tightly to things that aren't even there any more?

This will take many years of practice, but the good part is that just a little understanding will go a long way to developing your life and helping your happiness to blossom.

HAPPINESS IS PATIENT

If you have patience and tolerance, then you can have a lot of things. By practising patience, you allow a space to very gradually develop that gives you at least a little room to think and to compromise with people or in situations that would usually make you unhappy. From a distance, even just the smallest distance to begin with, the whole scene will look much better.

People may behave wrongly in your view, in a way you find hard to accept because it doesn't fit in with your own wishes, desires and beliefs. You want everyone to be understanding of you, but you can't accept others as they are. If you don't try to be accepting, to give others a chance to live their own lives, this kind of impatience can become a great obstacle to happiness.

When you are in a difficult situation with another person, the main way to practise patience is to put yourself into the other person's shoes. Take a breath and remember that person is just trying to get along in their own life, and that they have just as much misunderstanding and attachment to their beliefs as you are feeling in the heat of the moment.

If you don't practise patience, then you are unable to control your anger when the time comes, and soon your happiness is covered over by negative feelings directed towards others, life, the universe and sometimes towards yourself. You fall into the trap of the blame game.

Contemplate your day-to-day life

- How do I deal with the things that are happening in my life?

- What are the things that trigger negative emotions in me?

- What will I try to do instead if such-and-such a thing happens to me?

This kind of contemplation gives you a chance to reflect on your emotions and how you might begin to practise reacting differently to the same old annoying situations.

Be-friendly-with-all-your-emotions reminders

- Don't try to suppress negative emotions. You need to acknowledge emotions to be able to then let them go.

- Remember that all your emotions are valid, but *you are not your emotions* – you are not anger, you are not jealousy.

- If you hold on to anger, you will burn yourself.

- Practise patience, every day.

A Random Act of Happiness

When you a standing in a queue, in the car, walking in to the office – you can be anywhere – give yourself just a few seconds to wish happiness to the people around you. Do it every day and in no time it will come as second nature and just like focusing on the breath, this habit of the heart will gradually increase the space you have in which you get to choose your emotional reactions to particular situations.

11

Stop Comparing

Comparison is the thief of joy.
THEODORE ROOSEVELT

When you look at your life and begin to evaluate your own sense of happiness, do you compare yourself to others? These days, people are always comparing everything to create some kind of order or league table. Even small children in their first years of education are tested and compared with each other. It seems as though we don't know who we are unless it is relative to others – better than him, not as successful as her. Status becomes a measurement of happiness. So if we are doing very well relative to others, then we think we are happier too.

We are taught that competition is healthy – that it is the best way to encourage us to strive and want to better ourselves and our circumstances; that it creates an environment of expectation that, in turn, raises standards. But I don't really understand how it can feel good to win when someone else loses.

The weight of comparison lies heavy on people's

shoulders. You might feel jealous of others, you may doubt yourself or your abilities and feel that you aren't quite good enough when you compare yourself to others. The quest for perfection, or trying to be 'beyond compare', eats people up inside because perfection is an impossible goal. Disappointment is inevitable.

DEVELOP MENTAL FLEXIBILITY

What is status? Why have we somehow made it a condition of happiness? After all, there will always be someone 'better' than us in our minds.

We think if we impress others in some way, then we will feel a surge of happiness. But when we begin to believe we are better than them, we become isolated on our moral high ground and deny ourselves the chance to fully connect and interact with them.

I remember when I went on our very first Pad Yatra, I could hardly move after spending the first day picking up garbage while walking through the mountain villages. The next day I was so stiff, it was hard for me to bend over to pick anything up, but I'll never forget that our bodies taught us such a great lesson that day. If we never bend down, then our bodies become very inflexible and stiff, and it becomes increasingly difficult to do so. And it is the same with our minds: if we do not practise bending down to look the homeless person in the eyes as we give them food or change, if we do not practise bending down mentally to meet the thoughts of the people we love, but just go about our day always thinking that we are on a higher level, then we will never know true suffering, we will miss out on many of the lessons life offers us and we will never know true happiness.

We are all constantly comparing, and yet we are all in the same boat, trying to get to the same place.

LEAVE THINGS BE

Do not judge. Let me mind my own business.

If we can release our minds from constant criticism, disagreement, worry, wishing that things or people might be different – if we can *leave things be* mentally, then we will be so much more comfortable. Developing flexibility in our minds gives us a great deal of freedom. I am not saying it isn't important to question or investigate, to be curious with our minds, but instead of investigating everyone else ('the problem with so and so is . . . '), we might practise allowing others to be themselves while we work on the person we would like to be.

Most of us can be busybodies and get on others' nerves. As a result, there may be low-level disharmony or, in more serious situations, we may fight with each other. In the worst cases, disharmony and disagreement lead to war. A certain degree of self-control or discipline is definitely needed, therefore, be it for the sake of individual peace or collective harmony.

I used to be a very angry little boy. In my eyes, no monk was good enough, no monastery was good enough – everything was in bad shape. My father always reminded me that I had to improve myself and change my attitude, and that this sort of inner improvement would make me happier and less angry because my overall perception would be more positive.

More recently I have tried to be less of a busybody while on the Pad Yatras. I remember one in particular where I saw others doing things that I didn't agree with: nuns using too much water and washing whenever they had the chance, monks eating too much, foreigners chatting too much . . . If I'd let all these things get to me, it would have been a horrible experience for me, so I said to myself, 'Come on, leave them alone; if it is not too much, let them have a bit of fun too.' Had I not done this, I could have ended up checking on everything they did – how they cut their potatoes, how they cooked their food or even how they pitched their tents. And I would have been so busy with what other people were doing, I would have no time to do anything myself.

In a way, it's because we care so much about others that we go around checking on them – out of kindness and concern we may tell them what to do and what not to do, even when this is not our role. So we always have to check ourselves.

Minding our own business is different from being indifferent or being ignorant. We should mind our own business when it comes to judging others, but should be helping whenever our help is needed. In a way, it's as though we are all parents for each other: watching our children from a corner when they are learning to walk, letting them fully use their potential, without interfering, but always being there to support them in case they should fall.

LIVE LIFE DARINGLY

When people sit together chatting, they tend to find it very easy to complain or criticise. It's very rare that they will praise others, especially those they don't like. I think the ego takes up so much of the conversation that they forget to be daringly different, daringly positive, daringly kind and daringly understanding.

We feed our egos to feel good fleetingly, but then we don't feel very good at all once the moment passes. We might temporarily feel part of the group, maybe even that we are united through our shared complaints, but ultimately complaints put up more barriers because our true selves aren't getting along – only our egos. Our egos get caught up in feeling superior, but then you might be aware of that feeling quickly fading – this is your true nature coming through. These are the moments when we have a chance to see the difference between ego and nature, so be daring and grab that opportunity.

A hero is someone who dares to live a happy life, conquering their ego and controlling those jealous, insecure or proud emotions that make us do or say things to hurt others. It's ok to make mistakes, but it takes courage to learn from them, to wish to be a better person. But with a willingness to improve, you will be walking your path, little by little. And one day, without even noticing, you will become a great and kind person.

What are your true values and interests?

Happiness belongs to the self-sufficient. ARISTOTLE

Taking the time to read a book such as this one is like meditation; it gives you a bit of space in which you can explore what really makes you tick as a person, what really matters. If no one else was looking, what kind of person would you like to be? If you let go of the need for praise or approval – if it didn't matter whether anyone noticed you or not – who would you be?

In Buddhist teachings we try to develop the human skills of patience and tolerance and we try not to be so busy with everyone else's business. At the same time, we develop our own values and interests by exploring how we really feel about life, the kind of person we would wish to be and what kind of actions will be a good match for those values. When our thoughts, words and actions are in union, we really get into the flow of our lives.

We can use the experiences of our day to explore our values, strengths and passions:

- Did we react the way we would like to in that situation?
- Would we like to develop an aspect of ourselves that we saw a glimpse of today?
- Are we living a life that really catches our attention?

How do you respond to criticism?

Do you tend to take criticism personally? Are you quick to jump to the conclusion that someone is being critical of you just because of something they said or did? Or perhaps you are someone who needs the praise of others to feel worthy and validated – to give you the security of feeling you are good enough?

If you feel very affected by either criticism or praise, you need to practise increasing your self-sufficiency. Become familiar with your own strengths so that you can feel good about yourself without the need for others to tell you. When you feel the first hint of criticism, try giving yourself a little space, so that you can see it for what it is, rather than immediately taking it to heart and feeling hurt. Is the criticism helpful in any way? If yes, that's great – take it as a lesson and a chance to grow or learn. If it has come from ignorance, then have the courage to look closely enough to see if there might still be a lesson there, while understanding that it may have little relevance for you and be more about the person who gave it.

Be aware that if you react very strongly to criticism, you may, in turn, be a harsh critic. If you can practise being less critical or judgmental of others, you will go a long way to being able to handle criticism with less drama yourself. If you are always striving for perfection, and feel burned when people point out the reality that of course you are less than perfect, practise patience towards and acceptance of other people's points of view. If you think someone is being rude to you, ask yourself, 'So what? Does it really matter to my life?' It's usually a case of misunderstanding, anyway. Even if the other person is very ignorant, you don't need to respond with ignorance or anger. Your beliefs and standards may seem exactly right and 'proper' to you, but they are just one set of labels. They are not the 'universal truth'.

I know that having 'good judgment' is something that many of us wish for, to feel proud of ourselves for having formed the right impression about someone or something or about a situation. 'I knew it,' we whisper to our egos, puffing up like a balloon so that we can hardly fit through the door. While it is important to listen well to our inner wisdom, it's useful also to be aware of the difference between wisdom and ego to let things be mentally, rather than judge and be critical. The Tibetans have a great saying for this – that it is easier to spot the fly on another person's nose than a horse on our own!

The space between

Clare has grown up with the belief that she is just a certain way, but is now gently releasing her self-beliefs and allowing a little bit of space to develop between external situations and her reactions to them:

People think I'm a very calm and relaxed person, and that's certainly partly the case. I have a wonderful job, family and friends. I have nothing to worry about really, and yet I am a worrier, especially about what people might think of me. I walk into a roomful of people and assume that no one will want to talk to me. I have always labelled myself as a shy and intro-verted person, but now my friends just laugh at this and remind me that I'll actually talk to anyone, so I must be the least shy, introverted person around.

I have realised that my perfectionism is my biggest block to authentic happiness. It makes me very quick to criticise others and also means that I am ridicu-lously upset when someone criticises me. Sometimes a person won't even mean to be critical at all – they are just pointing out how to do something. Or another example is that I will feel ignored when really people are just getting on with their own business.

Becoming an observer of my mind is just beginning to bring me a little understanding of what is going on in these situations. I am finding that I am able to reflect on why I might've got upset or been critical towards others, and let go of the associated emotions more quickly. My commitment to be less critical and less attached to my own sense of perfection is begin-ning to bear fruit – only very occasionally so far, but I know that with a lot of practice I will be able to develop the space between a situation occurring and my emotional reactions. It's not about losing my passion in any way or suddenly becoming a person who will never have opinions that differ from others', but I hope that I will become easier with difference and learn how to take the lessons of criticism if it's helpful and let it flow away if it's just saying more about the other person and not worth getting upset over.

THE JOY OF SATISFACTION

From my point of view, happiness is satisfaction. This might sound odd to some people – it doesn't sound very much related to pleasure or perhaps even joy. But for me, if I am satisfied with something, for example a relationship or the work I am doing today or the food I am eating, then I am happy, I am full of joy. This isn't the kind of satisfaction that comes from getting something or achieving a condition that I set before I allow myself to feel happiness, but rather, it is the relationship between me and my life as it is, right now. It is in the understanding that no matter how much external circumstances may change, it is my own perceptions that attach meaning to those circumstances. If I know I have tried my best, that my intentions have been good, then I can be more accepting of the things that I cannot be in control of, and I have the key to unlocking my own happiness and joy.

Some people might feel that success is the key to their happiness, and of course, doing well in something can help to make us feel very good. But I believe that happiness comes when we are satisfied – because if we are not ever satisfied then however successful we are, we will still feel like we have to keep going to the next level. We will never give ourselves a chance to enjoy or appreciate what we have in the present moment, we are constantly running ahead into the future.

Satisfaction can be confused with complacency, but they are not the same in my mind. Satisfaction does not mean that we sit back and think, Great, I can just put my feet up now because I am satisfied with my life. Satisfaction comes from joyful effort – it comes from knowing that today we tried our very best, from being adaptable to change and from truly appreciating the life and the love we have.

When we feel a sense of satisfaction we feel less of a need to cling to our success, relationships and opinions, and also we are less fearful of losing what we have, which makes life much more pleasant and easy. Instead of wasting mental energy in a state of anxiety, constantly comparing ourselves to others to check on our status in the world, we work with the one person we can influence: ourselves. Instead of demanding that our partner or our friends be a certain way, we try to be the most caring and loving partner or friend ourselves and let others be themselves.

A day free of opinions

For today, let go of opinions. Whether you tend to be critical of others or of yourself, practise leaving things be today.

1. If you are someone who is always being asked for helpful advice, take a day off and ask people what they feel they should do in their hearts, listening to their own inner wisdom.
2. If you are someone who likes things to be just so, have a live-and-let-live day.
3. Be accepting of other people's views and ways of being; you don't need to give up any part of yourself to do this — it's just a case of consciously putting yourself in other people's shoes for the day.
4. Be conscious of your words today, putting aside any urge to correct unless it is truly helpful.
5. Have a day free from comparison; be true to yourself and your own values.

THE GIFT OF SILENCE

Silence is a true friend who never betrays. CONFUCIUS

I am a great believer in jumping into the stream of life and going for it. However, I also believe that there are many lessons to be learned from being quiet. This is when we allow or encourage our minds to enter a more contemplative state and we can really begin to develop our insight.

It is so easy to waste time and energy with gossip, even while saying that there aren't enough hours in the day to achieve what we would like to. So instead of always talking, always looking outside ourselves, let's take the opportunity of silence to look inside. Don't be afraid of the quiet; don't be afraid of sitting still. Some people can't sit still even for a few minutes without feeling agitated and impatient to get up and do something, or at least compile some kind of to-do list in their minds. But it is in these moments that your inner self will stretch and grow, and so external life will naturally improve too without worrying about it so much.

We cannot control what is on the outside, whether it is the thoughts, words or actions of others, but we can take a little time to explore how we are developing ourselves as a person. These are the moments when we can check in on our intentions and motivations and ask ourselves if our own words and actions are matching up. We can remind ourselves of all the things we have in our lives to be appreciative of, we can acknowledge our emotions and even the things that are upsetting us – we can accept them and allow ourselves and our lives to move on.

Watch one's own mind as it is definitely the guru.
MILAREPA

Our mental attitudes, if we are not careful, may build a wall around us. This might create obstacles that prevent us from forming meaningful relationships (and really, isn't that what life is all about?). Flexibility is the key: don't be so quick to criticise or disagree, just leave it. Don't talk too much about others; this is a source of so much negativity. When we speak negatively of others, then we are also having negative thoughts. How can this help when it comes to our happiness?

If you don't feel comfortable with someone else's way, that's fine, do it your way; but likewise, you don't need to impose your way of being on to others. Celebrate difference. See other people's strengths, rather than being quick to point out the things you think they need to improve. Do what's in your heart and encourage others to do the same.

Stop-comparing reminders

- Remember that you are already good enough
  – your nature is beautiful, you don't need to be
  better than anyone else and you don't need to
  worry that others are better than you.

- Practise leaving things be. Let others be themselves – who are we to judge? – and let us
  concentrate on improving our own minds and
  our own lives instead.

- If no one else was looking, what kind of person
  would you like to be? How can you develop that
  aspect of yourself; what can you do today?

- Be daring enough to stay away from gossip or
  complaints and your happiness will find you.

A Random Act of Happiness

....

Plant a tree: a few years ago we created a
fantastic tree-planting event, when we broke
the world record for the number of trees
planted in sixty minutes. It was the best day,
and I don't think I have ever seen so many
happy faces.

I have a deep love for trees. They give
us so much: they protect our hillsides from
mudslides that destroy whole villages; they
make the air that we breathe healthy; they
provide fuel and furniture and even the paper
on which this book is printed; they give us
beauty – from the majestic oak to the wiry
eucalyptus and the mountain pines. They fill
up our senses . . . so if you ever get the
chance, plant one; plant as many as you can.

12

Develop Meaningful Connections

There is a net of three dimensions, vast and wide, stretching in all four directions throughout the universe. At each point that a string meets another point of the net there is a jewel, and this jewel reflects in it all the other jewels of the entire net, and further that reflection too is reflected in all the facets of the other jewels.

No single part of the net can be independent of the rest; a single movement of the net in one place will affect, in some way, the most distant part of the net or universe. The all is reflected in the one, and the one in the all. THE FLOWER GARLAND SUTRA

If you were to ask me directly what is my happiness, it is in interaction and connection, because everything in life is interconnected and interdependent. We are not an island, we live side by side with people and all kinds of living things every day, and so to cut ourselves off and live in our shell would mean that we are missing out on so much that this precious life has to offer. As a friend of mine says, if we live in our shells then we are nuts – 'Don't be a nut!'

So, for example, happiness for me is to go deeper into the connection with my friends. We might be having a conversation, and in the beginning we think about whether the other person is nice looking or a nice person, whether we agree or disagree with what they are saying, what we are going to say next. We might even be somewhere else entirely in our minds, thinking about the list of things we need to get done today or a conversation we had with somebody else. What kind of happiness is going to come when we are so easily distracted, when we find it so difficult to be still in our minds and our bodies and pay attention?

However, gradually, through intention and then practice, which is really developing our sense of awareness, we calm these surface thoughts and begin to make a connection with the other person on a deeper level. We feel an energy transferring between us, we begin to sense how to put ourselves into their shoes and see things from their point of view. We get the chance to learn from each other.

And for me, the great sense of happiness comes when I go even deeper into my friends, right into their hearts, where I am lucky enough to see their beautiful nature.

It is a process of practice, rather than something that just happens as if by magic without any conscious thought. In my younger days I would struggle because I always got carried away with the superficial things, such as how attractive or young and energetic a person might be. Now – maybe because I'm getting old or maybe through training my mind – I have a bit of time to 'come down' and get into the heart of happiness.

When you open yourself up to developing deeper connections with people it is always rewarding, but it isn't always easy, as it is through the eyes of others that you see your own flaws – your unkindnesses, lack of courage or petty jealousies. You see everything you would like to work on in technicolour and that can be painful to begin with. But I encourage you to stay with it, because in your imperfections lies the possibility to transform your life.

LOVE

There are two basic motivating forces: fear and love. When we are afraid, we pull back from life. When we are in love, we open to all that life has to offer with passion, excitement and acceptance. We need to learn to love ourselves first, in all our glory and our imperfections. If we cannot love ourselves, we cannot fully open to our ability to love others or our potential to create. Evolution and all hopes for a better world rest in the fearlessness and open-hearted vision of people who embrace life. JOHN LENNON

Love is at the heart of happiness; if we let it, then love may be at the heart of everything we think, say and do.

Love is so helpful when it comes to bringing us back into the present. We are focused, generous, kind and joyful. We have to be brave and jump in, not knowing what will be around the corner. We have to trust in love, in others and in ourselves. Love gives us so many lessons on happiness! Love needs our care and attention to flourish and thrive – just like our minds and our lives; if left untended, it can soon grow wild and out of control, or lose its richness, vibrancy and colour.

Of course, love for a partner goes hand in hand with desire, and so it may be helpful to check ourselves to understand how we may be devoted to another person without clinging to them. We may love unconditionally and generously without imposing demands on that love. This is a type of fearless loving, where we give happiness without the expectation of receiving, because in giving we receive anyway.

Loving relationships are a source of much happiness in life, but sometimes great unhappiness too when it seems like love breaks down. Love makes us vulnerable, we open ourselves up to the world, we make an incredibly deep connection with another, but if we sense that love is taken away, we can feel rejected, lonely and that life is cruel.

Still, I agree that it is better to have loved and lost than never to have loved at all. Wherever there is love in your life – not just romantically, but family love, friendship, love for nature or for what you do – try not to weigh it down with your own needs. These are the needs of your fragile ego, not your nature. They are the needs that reinforce your limiting self-beliefs. Nourish love with your kindness. If it ever feels like the connection is only one way, then rather than shout or scream, put all your great communication skills to use and gently investigate why this might be so. We don't have the power to change others, but we do have the capacity to understand before deciding the direction in which it is truly best to go.

FRIENDSHIP

If you want to go fast . . . go alone. If you want to go further . . . go together. AFRICAN PROVERB

As you know, happy time passes away so quickly. Therefore, we should appreciate every connection that we have made and try our best to enjoy each other's company. After all, we will have to part one day, one way or another.

Sometimes I worry that such great responsibilities have been given to a carefree and disorganised person like me. The lineage is too beautiful and too heavy for one incapable person. It is so good, therefore, that I have such great friends – that we are there to support each other. Even when I was young, there was a very special relationship between myself and my friend the late Drukpa Yongdzin Rinpoche. Even though he was very naughty, he never allowed me to be so. He always said to me, 'If you do what I do, I will not see you in this life and lives to come.' It meant so much to me, that he wanted us to meet in our next lives and continue to support each other. He wanted me to look after the lineage so that would be possible. What a great friend.

Our good friends give us so much through their friendship, we have to really cherish them. They give us support when we are struggling with our pain and suffering, and friends who understand us can help to shine a light on the way forward when we're fumbling around in the dark of indecision. Friends help to keep us balanced, they bring out the best in us, which helps bring us closer to our true nature and our happiness.

OUR TEACHERS

I have come to believe that a great teacher is a great artist and that there are as few as there any other great artists. Teaching might even be the greatest of the arts since the medium is the human mind and spirit. JOHN STEINBECK

Good teachers who have a passion and a love for teaching that comes out of their own experiences are a gift to us as individuals and to the benefit of all. We can respect and trust in the words of a good teacher or mentor and, as a result, we will be more inspired to act, rather than constantly question. Some people do not like the idea that they might need a guide along their path, and would prefer to find their own way without any help. But if we remember that it is always up to us to choose our direction, then we may benefit from the wisdom of others as we go along our way.

I was once asked why people find it so hard to make a change to become more environmentally friendly and I think part of the reason may be there are not enough really great teachers on this subject. Because of this, few of us are truly inspired to make a genuine connection with nature and take better care of it.

Life is our teacher

We need to give ourselves the space to learn, to open up and allow ourselves to listen and contemplate the lessons that life is offering us every day through good teachers, but also through our friends, loved ones, colleagues or bosses, people we interact with on the street and through nature itself, our environment and our community. Life is an incredible teacher and learning is such a wonderful part of life.

I'm very happy to forever be a student; I would like to try and be a good student for the rest of my life. Every moment there is the opportunity to learn something, but if we don't give ourselves the space to be students, we will miss out on so much. Every interaction that I have – every conversation or moment of connection – makes me happy because it is a chance to learn. The subtleties of energy that flow back and forth between people, between all beings and between us and nature are quite amazing. Give it the chance to flow by itself – it is such a beautiful thing.

RECONNECT

If you can develop your awareness and begin to see how you connect and interact with the world around you, then you are also getting to know yourself better. Right now, there is a big disconnect between how people perceive themselves, their intentions and their actions and the consequences of such actions on other people or on the world itself.

If you take the environment (a particular passion of mine) as an example: people no longer see how their actions make any difference, though of course, even the smallest change helps. A person might have the intention to be more environmentally friendly, but when they are thirsty they buy water in a plastic bottle without a moment's thought. Or perhaps there is a slight hesitation, but their motivation to change isn't strong enough and falls at the first hurdle. If you really want to *change your mind*, then come to Nepal and see what has happened to our pristine rivers and glaciers, littered with plastic bottles. And feel the smile on your own face as you pick up those bottles and make a beautiful river clean again. I think it is the same the world over – people who are cleaning up their local beach or park always look so happy. And this is just one example of why it is so important for our own lives and development that we nurture our connections with the world and the people around us. When you respect your environment, you respect yourself.

Happiness is a chain reaction

When we understand that all of our thoughts, words and actions are linked in a chain reaction, we begin to appreciate just how much each of us affects the people and the environment around us, and likewise just what an effect they have on us. So do we want to affect people in a positive way or in a negative way? The choice is always ours to make; it's up to us what kind of energy, or as we say 'karma', we want to give to the world.

People lock themselves up, always wanting silence, isolating themselves in the search for peace and calm. But if we cannot learn to have peace of mind when there is chaos around us, our minds will be very easily agitated. We will become angry at others for disturbing our peace. We will be irritated at the smallest fly or noise, so that our chances for peace of mind become slimmer and slimmer, as we have placed too many conditions on something that we could have at any moment, regardless of what is going on around us.

When we live only with ourselves – only in our own minds – we live a life that is only in our imaginations, and which cannot be shaped and changed by the present moment; in a way, we can't really live in the present unless we let ourselves interact with the world with all of our senses. If we live only in our imaginations, we will tend to cling to our view of the world, believing that our opinions and thoughts are the only truth and reality, rather than one person's perception or interpretation. So the more we interact and make connections, the more chance we have to see that while we might not all see things in exactly the same way, we are all in the same boat and all hoping for happiness in our lives.

Your happiness never relies on others

Generally, we would all like to keep our relationships as positive and as loving as possible, but we also know that many obstacles seem to come up that put our happiness in jeopardy. Sometimes we even find it difficult to continue with certain relationships. In the beginning, we become friends because we easily see the positives in one another and feel, 'How fortunate we are to be friends!' Then, as we become closer, our emotions come in the way. This happens with couples and friends and between teachers or gurus and students.

It's amazing how much we allow other people to affect our own happiness. Of course, it is understandable that when others appear to be deliberately hurting us we feel our happiness is threatened. But there are also many times in our lives when we fall prey to misunderstanding – when we get upset about a situation that might easily be seen from a different angle. We think others are out to upset us when they are really only concerned about their own happiness or success. But even that annoys and frustrates us: why can't they think about us a bit more? Why can't they be more sensitive to our feelings?

This kind of thinking restricts us and limits our potential for happiness. We end up in a pattern of negative thoughts: questioning why they aren't more sensitive – perhaps they don't love or respect us quite enough? – and then wondering what's wrong with us to have made them behave this way.

All this analysis starts to clog up our thinking. *If only they would just . . .* then we'd be happy. But when we start to rely on others for our happiness, then we are also relying on them, in a way, for our sense of worth – our confidence and self-esteem. So if we can begin to develop and cultivate contentment which doesn't depend on the words or actions of others, then we no longer need people to be a certain way; we can be like a tree that is able to sway in the breeze while having a strong foundation. If we can develop a stronger connection with our own wisdom and strength, then our relationships with others will be free from demands and conditions, giving us many more opportunities for happiness as a result.

DON'T TAKE RELATIONSHIPS FOR GRANTED

One of the main obstacles between us and our happiness, as I see it, is a lack of rejoicing in each other, in really appreciating each other. In other words, we begin to take each other for granted and then rejoicing is gradually replaced by annoyances and upsets. But if we are able to always rejoice in each other, this is a very good way to develop our understanding – you could call it a small step towards enlightenment and one step closer to our nature.

I have had the good fortune to keep positive relationships with my Gurus, my Dharma brothers and sisters and most of my students and friends. Of course, since nothing is perfect, some of these relationships do turn sour or negative. But I would like to believe that I try my best to keep all the remaining relationships with sincerity.

Try your best to rejoice in all the good things others are doing. Rejoice deeply with positive motivation, with the attitude that 'One day, I will follow his or her example to do good deeds,' rather than thinking, 'I wish he or she did not do such a good job, so that I could always be the better one.' Rejoicing is the best medicine for jealousy and it has a beneficial effect on your own inner confidence too. Why not give it a try?

IF A RELATIONSHIP HAS BECOME NEGATIVE

If you cannot cope with some of the people around you, you have to keep yourself away from them. At the same time, you should keep checking yourself – whether you are a negative or positive friend for others. You have to be very honest with yourself to know if you are being a good friend or a good person to another or if this is a relationship that tends to bring out the negative in one or both of you. Looking this in the face takes courage, but will often bring benefit in one way or another to everyone concerned.

Don't use my words here to judge others, however; this is to remind you to always look into yourself, to look into your own mind. Spiritual practice is for *self*-improvement!

Think of all the meaningful connections in your life; here are some, but what are yours?

- Gathering with friends for a meal

- When individual voices come together, connect and form a choir

- Co-ordination, working with others; happiness is in teamwork

- Devotion to your partner without holding them down with your attachment

- Connection with a line of poetry, a song, a work of art

- Connection with nature – that feeling as you walk beside the sea or through the park on a summer's day

- When you bend down to look into another person's eyes and see their suffering

- When you look into another person's eyes and see their joy

Value your connections and develop a sense of honesty with yourself. Think about what is happening in the world and also whatever situation you are personally going through. You may be secretly going through all sorts of ups and downs, but don't keep this secret and hidden from yourself – bring it out into the open and contemplate what is going in your life. Allow yourself to look deeply.

Connection is a pathway between you, the world and the people around you. Connection is a pathway for happiness.

Develop-meaningful-connections reminders

- Remember that everything in life is connected – happiness is a chain reaction.

- Don't isolate yourself, but develop the connections in your life.

- Look into the nature of those around you and see their beauty.

- Let love bring you back to the present and remind you what really matters.

- Cherish your friendships and let them cherish you.

A Random Act of Happiness

....

Write love letters: receiving a love letter is a wonderful gift, but perhaps even luckier is the person who writes and offers their heart in words. To write a good love letter you have to think carefully about what you're going to say, you have to listen to both your own heart and to theirs and you get to appreciate that person all over again, from the smallest detail to their whole being.

Allowing ourselves to care so deeply about another is a source of inspiration, a driving force for the everyday and for life. We delight in the detail – a smile, how their eyes light up with love or laughter, a meal we enjoyed together, the cup of tea brought first thing in the morning. We are reminded of a touch, a look, and pettiness fades away as it should, leaving just love in its place.

13

Allow Your Heart to Be Broken

You cannot protect yourself from sadness without protecting yourself from happiness.

JONATHAN SAFRAN FOER

Happiness walks hand in hand with all the other emotions that we experience. If we allow ourselves to care very deeply, whatever the emotion, then we take a step closer to being the person we are meant to be. When we pick ourselves up from a broken heart, we are a more beautiful human being as a result. It is essential that we do not ignore our sadness or pain. We don't need to wear it as a badge of honour, as that is the type of armour that will keep happiness from entering our hearts too, but we need to acknowledge all our emotions because it is by first looking them in the face that we are then able to let them go.

WHEN SAD THINGS HAPPEN, THROW OPEN THE CURTAINS

Your joy is your sorrow unmasked . . . The deeper that sorrow carves into your being, the more joy you can contain. KAHLIL GIBRAN, *THE PROPHET*

When the rug is pulled out from beneath us and we experience the pain of a difficult fall along the path of our lives, we have a choice whether to use this as a wake-up call or take an emotional pill and wish we could sleep and take the pain away.

If we choose to stay with ourselves and our emotions at these times, and try our best not to run for cover, then we will have a chance to become truly awake in our lives. Never be afraid to ask for help when you need it, just as you would want someone you cared for to ask for support from you. Never be afraid that you can't catch yourself if you fall – you just need to trust and give yourself the kindness and compassion that you give to others in a heartbeat.

Suffering, sadness and grief are an essential part of what it is to be human; they are even an essential part of happiness in a way. We can find the lessons in the challenges that we face, discovering strengths, perhaps, that we never knew we had or deciding to make improvements in ourselves. They remind us that life matters and that we shouldn't waste a minute; they are a part of developing a deep appreciation of life. So never be afraid to be sad or to grieve – have the courage to let your heart be broken, but then also develop the part of you that is joyful and loving, so that you won't ever be trapped in your suffering.

Again, it is by taking care of our minds that we can do this. We can feel all of the emotions of life deeply and fully. For example, the space that we give to our minds through meditation helps us to become better friends with our emotions, which sometimes means letting them be.

Just let go

This extract is from Trevor Stockinger's blog, 'Burning the Incense at Both Ends'. It is so easy to get caught up with the 'shoulds' and the 'oughts' that we can forget to listen to our own hearts and follow our own paths. Sometimes the bravest act of all can be to 'let go':

> Just let go is an often heard spiritual platitude. Yet, there is wisdom in this phrase. We are projecting upon the world our own expectations and view-points. When the world does not conform to our mindset (which happens all the time), we suffer a loss. Frequently, however, we fail to grieve that loss and accept it.
>
> It is easy to understand grief when a close relative or friend passes. We expect our close relatives and friends to be with us our entire life. We had plans with them and looked forward to their continued companionship; or we had conflicts with them that

we hoped we could resolve in the future. When they died, all of these expectations were shattered by reality. We had to go through the grieving process to come to terms with the loss. In these moments, our deepest heart knows that we need to let go and accept the change. There is no other way because death is the only certainty we have in life.

On a smaller level, losses happen all the time. For example, I received a text message from my mother. It expressed a viewpoint that was not consistent with mine and that fact startled me because I expected a different response. Immediately, I became angry. Then, I felt guilty because of the anger that arose. Finally, I settled down and accepted a new reality.

All of these emotions came up because I was grieving for a loss – a loss of the reality I had created. And, this is happening all the time. We like to pretend we are different from children who cry when their ice cream cone falls on the ground. But, really, we are all suffering these losses regularly. We have just developed coping mechanisms to avoid crying. Sometimes these same coping mechanisms, however, prevent us from grieving and letting go entirely.

Here's an example of what I mean. Over the last decade, I have worked with demanding perfection-ists. I have sought to meet their demands and to be the perfect lawyer they envision. I habitualised the need to stay up late, to put my social life and health aside to reach the goal of being a perfect lawyer. I took on their vision as my vision. Let's face it. It wasn't hard to do. I was a demanding perfectionist, myself, before I even met them.

A few years ago, having worked ninety-hour weeks for several months, I finally recognised that the cost of getting an A was not worth the suffering, and for the first time I told myself that it was okay to get a B or C.

But, since then, I have never fully lived that way. I am still attached to a perfect view of myself as a lawyer. I have not truly let it go of that ideal in order to live in a more healthy manner. Thus, conflicts arise. Anger comes up when the new way I am trying to live conflicts with the old perfect standard. Guilt arises for feeling angry. There is a muddle of emotions when trying to make change.

Change means loss – and we need to grieve that loss even if what we are losing was bad for us. Then, we can let go and move on.

This is why the spiritual path can be difficult. We lose our comfortable touchstones. We lose our pretences. We lose our conceits that lasting happiness can be met by altering our external world.

On the other hand, the more times we cry when the ice cream hits the ground, the stronger we'll become. We'll see that the world is just that way. Sometimes we get the ice cream and sometimes we do not. Either way, we can be content. At that point, we have truly let go.

BE PREPARED

At times people think I sound negative or pessimistic because while talking about happiness I will say that we need to be prepared for the worst and lower our expectations a little, which goes against the popular precept that we should always reach for our dreams and only look on the positive side of life. But my concern is that the sheer pressure to achieve is putting a massive weight on people's shoulders, and that far from being happier, they are becoming more vulnerable to mental conditions like depression and anxiety. It also means that we aren't prepared for the changing nature of life: we want all the ups, but lack the coping tools for the downs. Similarly, if we prepare for the fact that we are going to die – given that this is the one certainty we have in life – we will be much more likely to make the most of our lives and have the best chance to uncover our happiness.

In the Buddhist philosophy we talk of 'samsara' (suffering) and 'nirvana' (peaceful bliss) being like two sides of the same coin, both existing at the same time. In the same way, where there is darkness, there is always light. So when I say you should be prepared for the worst, this doesn't mean having a negative outlook or attitude; it is simply that you should be free from expectations – flexible and open to whatever the day may bring. A free mind is prepared for anything, but can also take you to places perhaps you never thought possible.

WHEN OUR HURTS TRAP US IN THE PAST

Once there lived a rich man's wife who gave birth to a beautiful little girl to whom she naturally became very attached. One day the girl died suddenly and her mother was stricken with grief. Nobody could console her – not her family or her friends. They tried everything they could to give her comfort, but she wouldn't let go of her little girl's dead body.

The story goes that the Buddha was passing by while this was happening, and so when he heard about it he wanted to try and help in whatever way he could; the mother begged him to bring her child back to life. The Buddha asked the mother to go and fetch a particular type of seed from a house in which no death had occurred. This type of seed was extremely common and something every kitchen would have, so the mother went away thinking she would soon return with the seed. She came to a house and asked the people there if they had a seed that she could take back to the Buddha, so that he might bring her little girl back to life. They said of course she could have a seed; but when she checked that no one had died in the house they replied that they were very sorry but their mother had died there a year before. The mother carried on from house to house; they all had seeds, but nowhere could they say they hadn't had a death in the family. When she returned empty-handed, the Buddha cried with the mother and explained that this was the nature of human mortality – that every one of us would experience death in the family at some point, and that although it was extremely sad and painful, it is the same for all of us. Finally, the mother understood and was able to put down the load of her daughter's body, and in so doing, she was able to let go of the burden in her mind and her heart.

How is it possible to stop past hurts from blocking our way? It is understandable that you might want to protect yourself, even subconsciously, from the same hurt happening again. You may find that you have put up a wall around your heart or your mind – whether between you and other people or between you and possible experiences and opportunities. You ask why you can't seem to find love, yet inside you are so frightened of letting yourself love because in the past you've lost people you loved. Try, if you can, to see your pain and fear from a different angle. If you're so frightened of losing love again, then surely it must be a very precious thing. And if it was a very precious thing, then that shows just how much capacity you have for it. Surely it would be a shame to deny other people this wonderful gift you have to offer.

I have met so many people for whom a crisis in their life has either turned into an opportunity to go along an interesting, sometimes exciting, new path, or has been a reminder to simply make the most of life. At some point, we all lose those who are nearest and dearest to us, but we can make a choice to see something good in any situation, however small. A best friend who dies far too young remains in our hearts, and while sometimes there will be no answer as to why such tragedies happen, we can still feel them when times are difficult, willing us on, being our biggest champion.

SAVING RELATIONSHIPS

In our relationships, there is a great deal of happiness and they are a source of strength and encouragement.

But just as life is full of ups and downs, so are our relationships. One day they might fill us with joy, but the next day a big misunderstanding occurs and we feel cut down. It matters to us that our friends or loved ones see us in a good light, and when we sense that they are looking at us and not liking what they see, we might either retreat into our shells and worry ourselves sick about how we are perceived, or we might go on the offensive and launch a few verbal arrows of our own.

To regain our balance is key, but the way that we will find this is neither through self-loathing or trying to get the other person back. Because as much as we might feel hurt by another's words, looks or actions, we will never regain our balance or happiness by looking outside for them or by going to the other extreme of becoming stuck in negative thoughts, whether about ourselves or others. Remember that misunderstandings come from people's perceptions of each other, when the wires have become crossed. If someone thinks we are this, that or the other, it doesn't become some kind of eternal truth about our personality. Everything in life changes from moment to moment, and while one day we might feel very hurt and upset, it will not last because our perceptions will change once again.

We can take the lessons offered by these experiences without holding on to any sense of blame or guilt, and we can get to know the ways which help us to get back into balance within our minds and our hearts. This might be through mind techniques like meditation, but equally you might balance the body to help balance the mind through therapies like massage, reflexology or exercises like yoga. For me, I might say the best thing is to go and walk in nature, if you are close to the beauty of nature it will bring you back to your senses.

If we end up losing a relationship because the hurt between us and the other person is too big, then we should not fight the feelings of sadness – we should allow them to flow, rather than hold on tight to them because life will come back up again if we allow it. Of course, there will be times when dark clouds cover up our happiness or our peace, and we may feel very agitated or uncomfortable in our bodies and minds. But if we allow the clouds to move on their natural course, we will be able to get back into the flow of our lives. We may need time to grieve and understand our feelings or our loss, but we should not live with regrets or infinite 'What if?' questions.

The silver lining of those clouds is that when faced with losing something or someone, we are also given the opportunity to appreciate that which is not lost. We reach out to those people who give us love and support and we say thank you for being a part of our lives. We might look at our parents, for example: even if we have grown apart over the years or we tend to fight with them, we can take a step back and think about how they probably did their best for us and that although they might not be our idea of perfect parents we can still be thankful to them for our lives.

In Buddhism we try to think of every being as our mother because it was our mother who gave us life. And in times of sorrow it makes sense that people will think of their own mothers and reach out to them, either in their thoughts or by going to them and talking things through with them. During these times, even the smallest show of kindness is like a ray of sunshine for us; sometimes it might open up our sorrow even deeper, but it will also shine a light on our happiness.

Allow-your-heart-to-be-broken reminders

- It is essential that you do not ignore your sadness or pain – they are as real as your joy and happiness.

- You don't have to always 'keep it together' on the surface – have the courage to let your emotions come.

- Trust that you and those who love you will catch you if you fall.

- Know that if you can accept death, then you can really live.

A Random Act of Happiness

....

Ask your loved one what they need to be happy today: when you give a loved one something they need, unconditionally, with no need even for thanks, then your heart will be full of happiness: when they are tired, let them sleep; when they are frustrated, lend them the space you have in your own mind.

14

Give Today Your Full Attention

*Thus life passes, speeding towards death like
autumn clouds, dancers' steps, flashes of lightning
in the sky or waterfalls – constantly moving and
changing without pausing for even a single instant.*
LALITAVISTARA SUTRA

When we begin to contemplate the impermanence of
life, we are then truly open and willing to see as we
have never seen before. We rejoice in the detail and
as a result of this kind of thinking, our selfishness and
arrogance go down because we kneel in front of the
truth that *anything* can happen in the next minute.

When we are *present* in our lives, we experience a
new type of freedom. Our worries about what might
go wrong dissolve as we are taken up with the moment,
with being fully attentive in the here and now. This is
why it is so important to develop our awareness, our
mindfulness, so that we may appreciate *today* rather
than only think of the possibilities of tomorrow or how
we would change things if we could turn back the clock.

We are all superheroes

Jonathan has managed to turn one of the great downs of his life into something that has 'only brought positivity' into his life:

I have always had an adventurous spirit and from a very young age yearned to travel the world and live in exotic places – a deep-rooted desire for new experiences. It was this very desire that took me, at the age of eighteen, to Africa where, through travelling to eleven countries and meeting the most wonderful people, I realised how fortunate I was . . . how privileged I was to have choices. I didn't fully appreciate at the time what that meant, only that on the surface not everyone seemed to have choices.

Twelve years later I was diagnosed with HIV and I suddenly felt that all my choices – the very thing that I thought was my passport to happiness – had been taken away from me. It was this experience of realising and accepting my own mortality that allowed me to truly start to live my life, to appreciate every moment and savour every encounter, good or bad, and to see the joy in the tiniest things. What had seemed like a death sentence had become a beacon of light that through acceptance has only brought positivity to my life. There are so many situations in life that can feel like that moment I heard I had contracted HIV, like the world has ended, but then you realise that it didn't end.

As a boy, I always loved the idea of being a superhero, helping others and having special powers; I now see that we are all superheroes. We have the ability to make choices, to change the way we look, the way we feel and even the way others feel. We can't always change the circumstances or the world we live in, but we can change the way we live in it and create our own happiness.

COME BACK INTO THE PRESENT

A single gentle rain makes the grass many shades greener. So our prospects brighten on the influx of better thoughts. We should be blessed if we lived in the present always, and took advantage of every accident that befell us, like the grass which confesses the influence of the slightest dew that falls on it; and did not spend our time in atoning for the neglect of past opportunities, which we call doing our duty. We loiter in winter while it is already spring. HENRY DAVID THOREAU, *WALDEN*

Why are so many people trapped in the past in their minds? Why do we hold on to resentments or old hurts, allowing them to hold us back or take up so much space in our minds and our hearts?

There is a Buddhist story about a monk who is travelling with his companion. They come to a road that is almost impassable because of a mudslide and a woman is on the side of the road, unable to go any further. The monk offers to carry her across the road, so that she can continue her journey, for which she is greatly appreciative. But later on, the companion looks very perturbed, so the monk asks what is bothering him. The companion is very upset because the monk's status means that he should not be carrying a woman across the road like that – it really wasn't an appropriate thing to do. The monk smiles at his companion and tells him, 'Friend, I put down the woman a long time ago; why are you still carrying her?'

There is a tendency to carry so much in our minds that is past and unnecessary to hold on to. Thoughts of past and future are no more solid than a dream, and yet just like when we are asleep and caught up in our dreams we believe in these thoughts as though they are truths.

As a child, when your present was not pleasant you projected your mind into a brighter future. As an adult, through meditation and mindfulness, you can train your mind to stop jumping backwards and forwards and instead learn to sit and breathe and in exchange an internal, present happiness starts to grow.

Many people feel they went through an unhappy childhood, and that may be the case for you – but if so, that is now finished. As an older person, an educated adult, now on your own path, you have to try to investigate and ask the question, *Where is the real happiness?* The real happiness comes from when you calm down. Yes, it was covered up by bad or neglectful things that happened, but these were superficial things – they caused a great deal of disturbance on the surface, like rocks thrown into a lake, but now you have the chance to let the water become calm again and see beneath the surface to something that, despite everything, remains true and undisturbed – and that is your inner nature and your inner happiness.

Write your own story

If you are unable to let go of resentments, they may turn into harder grievances, like a knot that constantly sits in your stomach or in the corner of your heart. They will be like an incurable cancer. It's up to you whether you let this continue for the whole of your life or choose to turn it around.

So this is your chance, right now, to forget it. Let that chapter be over and start a new page, write your own story. This is your life. Every morning when you wake up is your opportunity to make a fresh start. You are free to be happy, if you want to be. Now is the time to do it. Don't wait.

It is very important to realise your happiness is always there, within you. It is your essence, and whatever comes and goes in your life, you can take strength from within yourself, and you can trust yourself. These are the things that I believe you sense when you allow yourself to really listen to what your heart is telling you. And this is why we have tools – such as meditation – to help us listen a little better.

You might only catch an occasional glimpse of deep happiness because of all the layers that have built up through the course of your life. And some of those layers won't dissolve in an instant, but if you are willing to try and look beyond them, that is a great start. This is why we encourage reflection and contemplation; why we take the time to stoke the fires of our aspirations and motivation. Some people may call it your inner glow, the peace within yourself, but whatever form it takes for you the first step towards happiness begins with awareness and attention.

WHEN YOUR LIFE HAS YOUR ATTENTION, MEANING IS NOT DIFFICULT TO FIND

Many people believe that meditation is used only to calm or pacify the mind. This is certainly one of its benefits, but if that is the only one we experience, then it would be difficult for meditation to have a positive effect on most of our day – when we are not meditating the effects soon wear off; and also, we will then only associate a peaceful and calm mind with the practice of meditation, rather than with the practice of our daily life.

It is therefore a good idea to think of meditation not only as a calming practice, but also as a way to become more aware of yourself. In this way, you will be able to merge meditation with daily life, rather than consider them to be separate. Be aware of yourself as you eat your breakfast, pay attention to your body and senses as you drink a cup of tea or talk with a friend. Don't be quick to be critical or judgmental of yourself if you don't always act as you would like to, but simply notice your thoughts, words and actions. This kind of awareness will not only deepen your appreciation of life and your connections and inter-actions with others, but it will also help you develop the meaning of your life. Because when your life has your attention, meaning is not difficult to find. Life is full of meaning, it is full of opportunity, and if you find the meaning of your life, it is difficult to be sad or depressed.

Mindful driving

Carol came to live in Kathmandu and soon discovered a lesson in attention on the chaotic roads:

A few years ago I was a typical Australian driver. The roads there are wide and spacious, but everyone is impatient, rushing to try and pass each other, frus-trated by slow drivers. It's like everyone is a terrible driver except you! And then when we retired, my husband and I bought a caravan, and in a moment I had to become a different driver. I had to slow down because the caravan wouldn't go any faster! So I sat back, and for the first time in the driving seat I just relaxed. I stopped pushing and enjoyed the ride a lot more. I didn't spend time worrying about the drivers behind me, who were probably going nuts, but I did send out prayers for them not to feel frustrated.

So having the caravan forced me to slow down, which made me realise you can't possibly watch out for your mind unless you calm things down a bit.

And then, a couple of years ago, we moved to a big, bustling city in Asia, where at first glance, the driving just seems insane, but after a while you realise it's a form of respectful chaos. Every driver just feels it is their right to get from A to B, and off they go. You can't wait around letting people in or you'll sit there all day, but equally every day I drive is a lesson in patience. I remember one day when I did bump into the back of someone. I had been on a four-lane highway, filtering into two lanes. Every time I tried to inch forward, someone would edge me out. It felt like I was going to be stuck on this highway all day and night, and gradually my frustration levels got higher and higher. I started thinking, 'But it's my turn now' and, 'This is just getting ridiculous'. I started to nudge forward, brimming with this impatience and immediately bumped into the car in front. It was only a cracked taillight, but in this city that means hours of waiting for the police and trying to negotiate the other party down from an extortionate amount of money to pay for a tiny repair.

I'm glad I did stand up for myself when trying to not be swindled by the repair costs, but the initial accident was a great lesson for me on just how important patience is, both when driving and in any difficult situation. I remember when I first got to here that I spent the first six months being driven by this great taxi driver; I observed everything I could and I was mindful of my initial reactions to every close shave. I practised calming those reactions; I still had them inside, but I no longer jumped every time a moped cut straight across us.

IT IS WITH AWARENESS THAT WE SEE ALL THE CONNECTIONS

Can we help ourselves or even train ourselves to be happier in the moment, to spot happiness when it is right in front of us?

If you want to be someone who is able to live in the moment more, then you can't just wave a magic wand and expect it to happen. You have to practise because this is something you do with your mind – and, as we all know, the mind easily becomes like a wild horse if we leave it entirely to its own devices.

As monks and nuns, we are fortunate in this respect because we are taught meditation from such a young age. But it is not just as simple as sitting on a mountain and praying, without any of the responsibilities of living in the real world; after all, I am responsible for hundreds of monasteries, nunneries and schools in the Himalayas, and for the wellbeing of the monks, nuns, students and many other projects. But the mind practices I have been taught over many years, and now have the opportunity to teach to others, mean that I am able to understand the pointlessness of worry or regret; that even as we make preparations for things that are still in the future or learn important lessons from the past, today is what really counts.

To live in the moment doesn't mean that we let go of our responsibilities; actually, we focus better on what we need to do to make sure we are looking after our responsibilities, rather than wasting precious time and energy on rumination and over-analysis of what has been or anxiety over the uncertainty of what is to come. When we dwell too much on either the past or the future we come out of the natural flow and rhythm of our lives, so that we might miss out on the opportunities of the present.

Let's say, for example, that I am a person who might be standing in the street and I want a cigarette. I tear the plastic wrapper off the packet, then pull out that little paper inside too and just throw them in the street, so I can get on with having my cigarette. I am not even aware of what I'm doing. It is just a habit, something I do without thinking – and especially without thinking of the consequences of my actions or anything beyond my desire to smoke. As long at the cigarette is in my hand, for that moment nothing else really matters to me. And the tragedy is in those words: *nothing matters*. If we aren't aware of what is going on around us or what is going on in our lives, how can anything matter? How can we care? Even something that seems like a tiny act of littering, when you think about it, is a very negative thing to do to the world, destroying the beauty, health and cleanliness of our environment.

This is why it is so important to always be learning and educating ourselves, so that we may just be a little bit more aware of how all of our actions have consequences – that *everything* we do matters. Some people may say that ignorance is bliss, and that those who don't care very much for others or for the world are quite happy in their ignorance. But for me, ignorance is definitely a form of suffering. How can we make deep connections and interact with the world if we are ignorant and full of misunderstandings? How can we develop the meaning in our lives? How can we be happy?

STRONG BODY, HAPPY MIND

Take good care of your mind, and also your body, so that each supports the other. I first began meditation training when I was about eight years old and I know that it has made a great difference to my life. It helps me to understand things a little more clearly and to be friendly with my own nature and thoughts, so that I have a sense of space that allows me to feel very comfortable and happy. However, to be honest, what has really given me so much strength in my life is putting love and friendliness into action. Teaching the villagers about what is biodegradable and what rubbish will remain in our beautiful rivers and mountains, polluting them, as we have been doing for the past ten years since starting the Pad Yatras, is a tiny thing in the grand scheme of the world, but it means I am able to put my love for the world into action and this is extremely strengthening for me. So while it is often a good idea to begin to get to know ourselves by sitting and contemplating, we also get to know ourselves and cultivate our minds and our happiness when we are *doing*, when we are really getting stuck in with life, rather than being stuck only in our thoughts.

Understanding the difference between pain and suffering

Apil, who joined the Indian pilgrimage, found she was able to perceive her own pain differently by allowing her mind to settle and be less quick to use the same old labels she had when the same health issues had come previously:

I had benefited so much from the pilgrimage with His Holiness in India. Events, teachings and thoughts which happened during this pilgrimage have since been deeply etched in my memory, and will remain so for the rest of my life. From the bottom of my heart, I thank every single person in the pilgrimage for that.

His Holiness's teachings on Appearance and Emptiness had left their imprint on me.

I have had to deal with my health issues for years, and regardless of the fact that they are non-life-threatening and for some, trivial – I took it really hard. When these ailments strike, everything in my life goes down with them. I would always be so absorbed in it that nothing else matters. This was the mode that I have been operating in for years.

I had to deal with these health issues during the pilgrimage and at first I gave in to them again. But I was reminded of His Holiness's teaching on 'appearance'. Was it my mind that had conjured the illness up to be more painful, undesirable and uncomfortable? What if I could be more accepting of the situation, treat my health issues as appearances that I could look at from alternative viewpoints rather than react in exactly the same way, with the same intensity each time?

It was astounding and for the first time in my life I fell sick happily. The ailment came and went, as it always did, and this time I went through it with a sense of calmness and acceptance. That was when I knew I had felt the incredible effects of distinguishing appearances from experiences. And quite honestly, I am looking forward to continuing these 'experiments' for the rest of my life!

When we make an effort to be strong in our bodies, this helps us to have strength in our minds too. I always think of the example of the small dog that is constantly barking, trying to make itself big and important despite its size, and the large, quiet dog that is full of strength and does not need to make any show about it.

In the same way, a relaxed, peaceful mind is much

more powerful than one that is buzzing away like a bee trapped in a jar (see p. 111). Emotions like anger, words of aggression and acts of violence are all just false shows of strength – like the barking of the small dog. The real power comes from a calm, unassuming and non-arrogant self-confidence. This is when you have a foundation of stability in your mind, you can trust yourself and stop looking to blame others too. You are able to take responsibility and understand that your mind is like a hero, and it's up to you how you put its strength, creativity and aspirations to good use.

Practising focus and attention is good for the mind *and* body. When you are distracted your intentions and actions are often not in unity – your mind is thinking one thing, but your body is doing something else. Or you are 'here in body, but not in mind', so you might be eating a very nice meal, but you are distracted by talking with your friends on Facebook at the same time or watching a football match on the television.

As a simple example, think about how tiredness might cause you to react very differently to a critical remark at work, in contrast to how you might easily let it go when you are feeling well rested and strong both in your body and mind.

It is a two-way street; the mind can help control the body's cravings. When you feel that craving for a sweet cake, the only thing that can come between you and your body's desire is your mind. And you can use the mind tools of meditation and awareness to cool your body when you feel the burning sensation of anger; you can mentally take a step back and ask yourself: do I want anger at this moment or would I rather choose peace? Likewise, you can create feelings of warmth and energy in your body through appreciation and reflecting on what inspires you, your intentions and motivations for the day.

It makes sense

Louisa sees the connection between mind and body in her work on a daily basis:

I am a yoga therapist and in the few years since I started investigating this philosophy I have found many tools that help me be of better service to my clients, and along the way to myself, too. I've realised that we never stop learning; there is never a moment to be complacent as that is when laziness creeps in.

The connection between body and mind is so present in my daily job. When I get a physical ailment I always ask myself what is going on in my head right now. It's the same for clients: they might come to me with a painful knee and just want an exercise to help it get better, but the mind is always involved, whether as an ingredient of the pain or of the healing process.

A big realisation for me has been the understanding that by working on ourselves and developing ourselves, we benefit others. I used to be an architect, which is a dream job for many but not for me. So I gave up a great career and salary and started from the ground up again as a yoga teacher and then therapist. Do what you love; don't waste a minute.

This all sounds very rosy, but I also have a good example to show just how much I am a beginner! I was on retreat, staying in a large room with women from many different countries. We are up at 5am to attend the morning puja (prayers) and then, after a day of teaching, the evening puja sometimes goes on for up to four or five hours. It's exhausting. Yet some of the people in my room would stay up talking quite loudly all night. I'll be honest – I could feel my anger rising with each hour of lost sleep. I was about to blow my top one night, but went for a walk to cool down and it was only when I came back – a little calmer in my mind – that I understood what was happening. One of the women was very ill with a chest infection and I had been woken by the sound of her friends trying to release the constriction by massaging her. I felt terrible that I may have glared at this poor woman who was really suffering. The next day I looked for her so I could give her a big smile instead.

Many people today have a growing understanding of how interrelated the health, and therefore happiness, of the mind and body are. If we feel good in our bodies, then we feel a little better in our minds, and likewise the opposite is also true. But we need to take this understanding further because I don't think many people see the intimate connection between the health of our bodies and the health of our environment – the nature that exists all around us. The mind needs the support of the body, and the body needs the support of nature to be healthy and strong.

We may use our minds to develop the understanding that if we don't take care of our environment, then we cannot be truly healthy in our own bodies, and so we can't support our minds and experience genuine happiness: a happy mind comes from a healthy mind, and a healthy mind is supported by a healthy body, which can only be healthy if all of the elements around it are healthy – if 'Mother Earth' is healthy. So if the trees are healthy, then we have oxygen; if the water is clean, it will give us life. This is all in our hands – what we do and how we lead our lives.

Developing an eco-friendly way of life is a crucial step in creating a better quality of life and so a happier life. For me, the person who looks outside of themselves to consider the health and happiness of their children and the future generations to come is truly wise and truly happy.

This is not a deep philosophy, it's a very simple way of looking at things, but it is so often overlooked. If we aren't willing to change our lifestyles in any way because we are worried about our personal comfort, then all the meditating in the world won't help us to be happier. We are good talkers, but we're not quite so good at putting our ideas into practice. And yet when we do I think we realise that this is where richness comes – this is where we feel like we have a fortune.

TAKE A BREAK FROM 'BUSYNESS'

Plenty of people miss their share of happiness, not because they never found it, but because they didn't stop to enjoy it. WILLIAM FEATHER

Like most of you, I am busy running around, always going from one programme to the next, struggling to find the time to sit still and be with my own mind. I try to remind myself all the time: 'Be grounded. Relax. Let it be.'

From time to time, I consciously drag myself out of the busyness and go for a train ride (I love the train rides in India) or for a walk. It is good to take a break now and then – to take it easy. Being ok or not depends on our state of mind, and for me, one of the top secrets to being ok in this chaotic world is to keep in touch with nature. While we can be very busy externally, we must always remind ourselves to be grounded in the heart, in the mind.

Being grounded – wherever we are – and enjoying and appreciating Mother Nature will bring more meaning to our lives and build a firmer and more profound relationship with our surroundings and the beings around us. This will also prevent our egos from demanding more from nature, leading to more natural disasters, which are becoming more frequent these days.

It is helpful to use such things as going for a walk or taking ourselves out of our usual environment to get our foundations strong and calm again. We don't need to be constantly zigzagging around, and likewise we don't always need to make mountains out of mole-hills when it comes to worrying about how life is going. But if we can allow ourselves just a little bit of time out to relax, then we can see things a little more clearly and with less drama. We can bring ourselves back into balance and realise that we don't always need to be chasing after the busyness of life and, instead, we can savour the peace of the moment.

Nature has a way of making us honest. When we are simply putting one foot in front of the other a great space seems to open up and we reconnect. When our feet touch the earth, we make a direct connection. We begin to appreciate, to be aware and to care, and we become free from fabrication and the usual nonsense that buzzes around in our heads. Nature is our refuge, our home, and if we begin to take better care of her, we will begin to take better care of ourselves. So perhaps now it is time to walk back towards her.

REJOICE IN THE DETAIL

If your state of mind is not comfortable, you don't have to stay with it. If you feel consumed by busyness and lack of time, or if you still feel agitated by emotions and situations that happened long ago in the past or by fears associated with how you imagine things might go wrong in the future, then always know that there is an alternative way – that you can take a more comfortable route. While it is true that your emotions are your teachers, you don't need to carry them all as you go through life. You don't need to hold on to things that made you unhappy in the past because what do they really have to do with today? Sometimes it may take courage to let go because, in a strange way, you might have got used to your suffering; it may be so familiar that you almost feel like you would be mentally naked without it; it is almost easier to keep the mental barriers up and feel like you know your limits, rather than open yourself up to everything the world has to offer.

When you are mindful of the detail, however, you notice the light come into the sky at sunrise, and how good the first sip of tea in the morning tastes. The detail will open you up to the happiness within that doesn't need grand gestures or for certain conditions to be in place. This kind of mindfulness is another reason for going on the Pad Yatras or taking time for retreat – because when you are walking in the Himalayas your mind becomes very friendly with the detail, especially with a hot bowl of food or a mat to sleep on at night. These simple things become the height of luxury.

Happiness is a jug of hot water

For Suzette, the simplicity of the washing facilities on retreat was the perfect reminder to appreciate whatever you may have in your hands today:

When I visit the abbey at Druk Amitabha Mountain I am struck by how much effort goes in to giving us visitors hot water so that we can 'wash body'. They heat large pans of water and give us a bucketful with a jug. As one woman said, if you're careful, then three people can get a hot 'shower' out of one bucketful! And in a strange way, I never appreciate a bath quite as much as those jug showers because you're so aware of where the water came from. Of course, I do appreciate the first bath when I get home, I'd be lying if I didn't say that! But the feeling of getting clean and warm with water carried up the stairs in a bucket is definitely a happy one.

If you are able, give yourself a chance to notice the detail in your life. Wake up early one day to watch the sunrise, appreciate your family as you sit around the table over a meal. When you go on vacation, rather than running around at the same pace, give your mind a rest from rushing, and a chance to see the world – and your life.

Often, it is easier to look at other people's lives than your own, to desire someone else's day. But you just end up missing out and getting lost in what-ifs, rather than being present in your life here and now, which is all you ever have. All the little things have to be noticed and appreciated; they are what makes life great and without appreciation life is just superficial, or as I call it, 'plastic' – we might end up like robots without senses, our hunger never satisfied, never fulfilled. When you bring your gaze much closer and stop looking over the fence you often realise just how much inspiration you already have to work with in your life. And equally, your life might inspire you to begin to make a change, whether it is to focus on something and really nurture it or to begin a new chapter afresh.

Be-happy-today reminders

- Being present in your life lets you rejoice in the detail.

- Uncover your happiness today – don't hold on to past suffering or old resentments.

- When life has your attention, meaning and purpose aren't difficult to find.

- Practise everyday mindfulness – savour each mouthful as you eat, drive with care, listen intently during conversations, notice everything around you as you walk outside.

- Take care of your body and you will take care of your mind – exercise makes you happy.

- Stop being so busy and focus on what really matters.

A Random Act of Happiness

....

Eat happy: there is a Latvian proverb that says, 'A smile is half the meal'. Food is so precious – it gives us life every day, it gives us energy, so why not give us happiness too? How much do we take food for granted? There are so many choices available to us, so many treats to grab. And how often do we search only for an instant sensory hit from food, rather than a deep sustenance? Happy eating is mindful eating – taking the time to choose foods that are good for our bodies, taking the time to cook for others and eat around a big table, full of smiles and chit-chat.

Part III

Putting Happiness into Action

Let experience take place very freely, so that your open heart is suffused with the tenderness of true compassion.

THE 3RD KYABJE DRUBWANG TSOKNYI RINPOCHE

My role in this life is to encourage people to nourish and cultivate happiness by developing themselves – how we actually go about the business of spreading happiness in our relationships, our work, our communities and taking care of nature.

I am very fortunate to be a student of the Buddhist philosophy, and to help people to put into practice some of those things that may help us develop ourselves, our connections and interactions with the world and our lives. After all, great thoughts and intellect will only take us so far – it is experience and action that really get to the heart of the matter.

It is a very attractive idea that if we have a happy mind, we will have a happy life. But as well as taking care of our minds, which is very important and really is the creator of a happy life, we also have to develop the art of *happy living*.

People are beginning to understand that if they take better care of their minds, this will help them along the path of their life. The tools of meditation and mindfulness are, therefore, becoming popular and, having used them for many years, I feel very lucky to have experienced the benefits they produce in terms of a more peaceful and calm mind.

What I hope for now is that people will take the extra step and put happiness into action in their lives on a daily basis; to add the art of living a happy life to thinking a happy life. The mind and the body can make an amazing partnership. We can use mindfulness to bring our attention into the present moment, to really feel what our bodies are telling us and, likewise, we can use action to clear out the clutter of our minds. For example, physical exercise is a wonderful happiness tonic for the mind. Contemplation needs to be followed up with action: we need to get into the flow of life and not always think quite so much about it. If we take ourselves too seriously we can end up stopping ourselves from jumping in and going for it.

If we are not careful, we can get so caught up in questions about what we should do or how we should go about something that we end up doing nothing. There are so many details and debates going on in our minds that we go round in circles getting tied up in knots and wasting our time and our energy. None of us ever knows exactly what the outcome of our actions will be or what is the 100 per cent best way to go about something, so while a little contemplation and discussion is needed, it is also a good idea to encourage ourselves to go ahead and take action, whether in our own lives or with something like taking better care of the environment. If we are able to create a balance of taking care of our minds, while also urging ourselves to act, then we will act well and without arrogance or pride.

Experience is the best practice of all. It is the best lesson. How can we really learn or understand without experience? That is why I always encourage people not to be afraid to try, because if you try your best, you will have a great experience. It is important to have the right motivation and intentions, but so many people have good intentions and such good hearts, yet feel afraid or unsure about jumping off the diving board and just doing it.

I am the sort of person who doesn't like people to talk too much, so that they may end up talking themselves out of action. You may spend your life buried in intellect, but it is only through experience – through *doing* – that you gain real understanding: you connect with your life and bring all your amazing ideas and intentions to fruition. You might have the odd stumble or wander off down a bumpy path, but you will gain strength from being able to stand up where you fall, and you will come across things you never thought possible down those 'wrong' turnings. Even when you take a very small step of putting your thoughts into action, I believe you are doing a great thing.

The easiest way to put happiness into action is to

share your own kindness and compassion; give happiness away and you will find yourself smiling at the same time. Then you might ask yourself, what would you like to give to the world today? What can you do today to help the world become a happier place? It doesn't matter how great an act, or how small, with enough individual drops of happiness you can fill an ocean.

15

Share Your Happiness

*It was only a sunny smile, and little it cost in the
giving, but like morning light it scattered the night
and made the day worth living.*

F. SCOTT FITZGERALD

Happiness is kind; happiness is loving and full of
compassion. There is happiness within gratitude, and
in giving. Happiness likes nothing more than to be
shared. And don't think that happiness is frivolous or
self-indulgent. If you think of it that way you are
selling it short – because happiness is powerful: it has
the ability to bring people together, to heal, to help
us do great things with our lives. A person who is
genuinely filled with the happiness and joy of living
is one who has a loving and sharing mind.

We, as spiritual practitioners, preach a lot about
'benefiting all sentient beings', which simply means
always acting with the benefit of others in mind. I am
sorry to say that sometimes I feel that we are not putting
enough of our words into action. We do our best with
the tools at our disposal for sharing ideas and practical

advice about how to help people spread happiness, love and compassion in the world, and look after nature and each other, but I don't know if we have done as much work as, say, the scientists and doctors of the World Health Organization (WHO) and CERN.

When I visited the headquarters of WHO I was so moved by the amount of *practical* effort the people there put into their work on solving some of the world's problems. And at CERN more than two hundred of the world's most respected scientists are working day and night on finding solutions to global issues. Yet when I visited their offices in Geneva I saw only smiles on the faces of everyone working there; I think this is because there is a very clear purpose in the life they live and in the work that they are doing for others. Happiness comes naturally when your life benefits others. This is a natural law of the universe. When we are able to benefit not only ourselves, but also other people, we have a glow that comes from within.

HAPPINESS SHARED IS
HAPPINESS DOUBLED

Whoever is happy will make others happy. ANNE FRANK, *THE DIARY OF A YOUNG GIRL*

By sharing happiness we cause our own to deepen. Sharing is a form of interaction and making a connection. As we share our happiness we get to know our own nature better and so we begin to create and cultivate the conditions in which our happiness will grow.

You might be surprised or even amazed at the impact your happiness has on others. This is easier to detect on an individual basis, when you see or feel an instant reaction, such as the return of a smile, but the energy and emotions that you share with the world all make a difference.

Just as a problem shared is a problem halved, so happiness shared is happiness doubled. What a wonderful thing to remind ourselves that happiness gets bigger the more we give it away. Really, we all know this to be true, but it's easy to forget as we travel along the bumpy path of life. When you walk along in the city you may notice just how many people seem to always be looking down at their feet or into the screen of a mobile phone. But then you see an interaction between people, or you might be one half of an inter-action yourself – a joke as you stand in line for coffee, a smile shared as you almost bump into someone – and you see how easy it is to spread happiness.

The gift of generosity

Miguel-Angel Cárdenas, a journalist from Peru, was lucky to understand a great lesson while on retreat with us in Nepal:

It was during the thirteen koras (circumambulations) around Swayambh-unath Stupa. There I understood the meaning of a pilgrimage, how the mind gradually becomes more present and more aware on that journey, which is an inner journey.

When I was doing the eleventh kora, and limping, I felt that I couldn't take it any longer. Going uphill, I fell down together with my backpack and bottle of water; I was almost lifeless. At that moment I turned around and there he was, the Gyalwang Drukpa! And he gave me one of those smiles of his, so full of light, comforting me.

I felt a tremendous energy. I stood up as if there were no pain whatsoever. Hundreds of people had begun doing the kora, and now only a few remained. And I felt as if I were in heaven, so blessed to be marching along towards enlightenment. But it was only my ego, still busy at work.

I walked the next two koras in a mystical state. At the last one, we had to climb those arduous steps towards the summit of the main stupa. I had an intense desire to be one of the few who made it to the summit, to be special in some way.

There on the first steps, I saw a Korean nun and she was grabbing her chest. She was a lot older than me and I had been amazed at her resistance up until now. But then my selfishness appeared and I thought to myself: 'Someone else will help her; I have to reach the summit with His Holiness and feel liberated.' I went up three steps and then I felt ashamed of myself and my thoughts, so I went down and offered my arm to help her.

My mind was still obsessed with wanting to reach the magical summit. I couldn't believe this was happening to me; a few minutes ago I was supposed to be blessed and now everything was being thrown overboard – so much effort for nothing. And the nun walked so slowly, one step took five minutes. My desperation was enormous. I helped her, although with some anger, with a heart full of black clouds.

Then suddenly, I became aware of this. It was the greatest teaching of my life. I became aware of what was going on in my mind, of the defilements, the ego and the black clouds. These were timeless seconds for which I will be forever grateful.

This was one of the happiest moments of my life, holding the arm of that nun with the smooth smile. We reached the summit without even thinking. When we were at the last step, accomplices at peace, we saw that he was there! The feeling wanted to make me laugh my soul to the sun – he was still there; the Gyalwang Drukpa was still walking around the stupa. Was he waiting for us?

It was such a beautiful experience. Today I remembered it at just the precise moment, just when I most needed it.

GENEROSITY IS UNCONDITIONAL

Happiness quite unshared can scarcely be called happiness; it has no taste. CHARLOTTE BRONTË

Never be possessive of your generosity, otherwise there will tend to be conditions attached to whatever it is you are giving away. For example, you might give a colleague help with a project, but then believe that in return they owe you a favour. Or you might give your wife flowers so that she will be nice to you in return. Of course, your wife might indeed be very happy to receive flowers – and really isn't that enough? Because if she is happy, then I'm sure you will feel happy too. It is a simple equation – you are happy, therefore I am happy – but I think it's one that works very well!

The more that we can practise unconditional generosity, the less clinging we are to receiving anything in return, and then we uncover a wonderful source of happiness. Don't think too much about it – just free your mind to give whatever your heart tells you. Give with no expectation that you will receive. Give simply for the sake of giving.

Your suffering is my suffering, and your happiness is my happiness. BUDDHA

Perfect generosity

Katie felt a moment of recognition during a retreat teaching:

His Holiness talked about 'stingy' giving in one of his teachings. It's a perfect adjective and I immediately pricked up my ears to listen more intently as I felt a huge wave of recognition at the words. What we are aiming for is 'perfect generosity', which is when you give and you truly neither require nor expect anything in return. It is giving with no strings attached, and that includes emotional strings. I will hold my hand up to acknowledge that most of my giving is of the 'stingy' variety. I will go back and forth in my head interminably trying to work out what is fair, but I have become so attached to my sense of fairness that I never really give with a free spirit. And I have realised that stingy giving will never bring happiness, so if I want to be happy in my generosity, which I truly do, then I'm going to have to practise.

The first practice might sound strange at first, but then it begins to make sense. You simply give from one hand to the other. I think of this as setting up a mental habit of giving that is just what it is, with no emotions or conditions attached to it. And then, you practise giving small things that you can easily afford, for example, we now have a money box in our hallway for small change for charity.

I still have a long way to go with larger things, but

I am more aware of my calculating mind and I am also listening more to my inner wisdom. Because ironically, my first instinct of what is fair is the answer I finally come around to after wasting so much time and energy going around in circles building up an attachment to something that in the first moment of listening to my heart I was completely happy to give. So I'm recognising the potential for 'perfect generosity', and this is definitely a case where practice is going to be needed to make anywhere near perfect.

TO GIVE IS TO LET GO

If you have ever longed to buy something, and then you finally do it, you might feel euphoric in that moment. You believe it is the 'thing' that has brought you this moment of great happiness, but then almost immediately it begins to fade. Perhaps it isn't the actual object that is the source of your happiness, but the release from the *longing* of not having it. Ironically, in that moment we suddenly become less attached to the object, even though we now own it.

When you practise generosity, you are practising freedom. There is a simple joy that comes with giving without condition or expectation. There might also be the feeling of release as in that moment you let go of selfishness, you are less concerned for your own desires and instead conscious of others. Buddha taught that if we notice that we are too attached to anything, we will benefit by the practice of giving it away. The most obvious examples are money and possessions, but equally, we can consider all of our limiting self-beliefs (see p. 67) and opinions in the same way. If we worry that we are stingy, we need to embrace the generosity of our true nature. If, through gentle contemplation and self-reflection, we understand that we have anxiety around issues of trust, then one of the best ways to reveal and grow trust is to give it.

Give respect

Give the people you are with today your full attention. Listen and be willing to see different points of view rather than clinging to your own. Be generous with your good wishes, show your appreciation of loved ones in any way that you can. Practise patience as you go through your day. These acts of generosity will give your mind a sense of lightness and space.

Give wisdom and inspiration

Whether you are a teacher, a parent, a friend or a colleague, there will be times when you can simply listen and times when you can offer your own wisdom. It's important not to let your ego take over in these situations, but to practise putting yourselves into the other person's shoes and helping them to see what is in their own heart. You might offer a different perspective on a dilemma, a fresh idea for approaching a problem or a healthy distraction.

BE GENEROUS WITH YOUR WORDS

Something that really makes me happy is to see friends and students getting along harmoniously and genuinely supporting each other through good communication and selfless, truly selfless, contribution. When we have retreats or programmes, people from many different countries and cultures come together; this takes so much organisation, but with mutual understanding and a great deal of communication, all the pieces of the puzzle somehow come together to make a wonderful experience for all.

Communication is very important, as I always say. Unless you lack communication skills, feel insecure or have some hidden agenda, you would probably be more than willing to share information when it comes to a public event in benefit of all beings. If not, then check your motivation: why is it so? Maybe you have very good reasons – who knows? But in most cases it is about fear that is connected with the ego.

Communication is a practice that cultivates harmonious relationships among people. With level-headed and non-emotional communication, everything will work nicely: let's put whatever is not agreeable on the table and sort it out without getting personal. When we free ourselves of being so attached to our egos and all of our own opinions, we can be very generous in our communication with others. We are free of gossip or spite, and even when we disagree we can do so with respect and appreciation that there are plenty more views in the world than just our own.

Take the time to talk to a friend, write a love letter; try never to let your words become arrows, but instead offer them as gifts of your love, kindness and happiness.

BE GENEROUS WITH YOUR ACTIONS

Let no one ever come to you without leaving better and happier. MOTHER TERESA

Through practising appreciation, building our daily awareness and generating our motivation we give ourselves the opportunity to become more generous in our thoughts, our words and in our actions. It might be as simple as having the awareness to notice an elderly or pregnant person on the train to whom you can then give your seat. You may become more aware of how your friends and loved ones are feeling and if they are in need of a shoulder to lean on. And, gradually, your awareness and appreciation of the environment around you may encourage you to give a little of your time or skills to help with a charity or cause that you have a great deal of respect for.

What would you like to give?

Are you overly attached to any of the following?

1. Opinions
2. Possessions
3. Money

Consider what really brings you joy in life and what causes pain or suffering in your mind. Do any of these things make you anxious, do they cause upset with others, do they make you carry around unnecessary negative emotions?

How can you loosen the ties?

Would you like your opinions to be less self-centred? Develop your empathy by giving someone complete attention as you listen to them. Watch your mind, you don't need to be thinking about what you're going to say next, you just need to connect with their words. Can you imagine the freedom from having fewer possessions, less clutter? Take a weekend to put some things aside and give them to a charity.
If you are attached to money, practise giving small amounts away regularly. Think of it as just giving, no strings attached.

A generous mind is a happy mind. So if you feel you would like to develop this aspect, start small, but start today. Only give what you can afford, but remember that giving is about so much more than money; you can give love, kindness, laughter and inspiration. You can give happiness. There is very little that is free in this world, but when you take care of your mind, you have all these treasures that you can share. You are so lucky!

Share-your-happiness reminders

- Always remember that happiness likes nothing more than to be shared.

- When you align what you do with what you believe, you will automatically become a very generous person as you will contribute so much to the world.

- Give unconditionally, expecting nothing in return – as soon as you place conditions on your generosity, you place conditions on your happiness.

- Watch yourself and become aware of the things you tend to become attached to, whether it's money, possessions, people or something like wanting to be right all the time. Whenever you can, give these things away from the bottom of your heart.

- Don't make grand gestures with your generosity, but give what you can, however great or small, and you will allow your happiness to shine.

16

Can We Make the World a Happier Place?

If we don't globally reflect on what a good human life is, then we are in serious trouble. NIC MARKS

Today we have the world at our fingertips, through technology, through travel. And yet we live in a world of extremes. There is extreme wealth for the few, but also great poverty for many. We are surrounded by 'progress', yet while rich countries see rises in health problems like obesity and depression, poor countries bear the brunt of hunger and climate crises. The gap is widening because the sense of disconnect is widening. We have to reconnect.

The relentless pursuit of individual happiness has tended to get the human race only so far, and I would like to say that perhaps it is time for an alternative pursuit: the pursuit of universal or collective happiness. We need to wake up to the fact that the way things are, the happiness of the few is bringing unhappiness to the many. How can one person's happiness be deep and genuine if it takes happiness away from others; if as the rich get richer, the poor get poorer and the planet is in dire trouble, which will affect whole future generations.

If we don't start helping the world in whatever ways we can, it is going to fall apart, and then where will our happiness be?

Buddha said that to end our suffering we have to understand it from the depths of our hearts, and it is only through walking the streets and looking our suffering directly in the face that we will have a chance to understand it. If we can then turn that understanding into action, then this is really developing life. Happiness really begins to grow when we align individual needs with universal needs: if we don't look after our neighbour's happiness, then our own will suffer too. Everything is connected, and none of the truly valuable things in life is selfish. The pursuit of happiness, therefore, needs to be collective, rather than purely for the individual. And the great thing is that once we understand and embrace this, our experience of happiness becomes deeper on a personal level too. Collective and individual happiness walk together hand in hand. As soon as you wish happiness to another person, you uncover your own.

SUSTAINABLE HAPPINESS

We know that true abiding happiness cannot exist while others suffer, and comes only from serving others, living in harmony with nature, and realising our innate wisdom and the true and brilliant nature of our own minds. NEW CONSTITUTION OF BHUTAN (JIGME THINLEY, FIRST PRIME MINISTER OF BHUTAN)

Happiness blossoms when we live sustainable lives – when we are always on the lookout for the ways in which we can give rather than take. The more we give, the more we have; whether it is time, love, forgiveness or happiness. When we find what it is that makes our hearts sing, we want to share it. If we start something that is good for the world, in even the smallest way, others will be attracted to our actions.

Can we begin to adopt ways of living that not only nurture our own happiness, but also nurture our environment for future generations? Can happiness be sustainable, rather than at the expense of others or the world? From my point of view, if we look at our lives and think about the ways that we might be friendlier – to nature, to other people and to ourselves – then we will not only live a great life, but a happy life.

For me, the example of the environment illustrates this point very well. We *talk* about being friendly with our environment, but we don't really make an effort to connect with nature. I wonder sometimes, if 'nature' had a fan page on Facebook, how many fans would it accumulate and how many of these fans would actually go out and communicate with real nature?

To love nature is to go out and understand nature, to appreciate it and educate ourselves about it. If we don't make this connection with our hearts, everything is just a superficial show. I have met so many people who talk about 'being environmental friendly' or 'being eco-friendly', but they don't even go out to understand nature. How do you make friends if you don't connect and if you don't meet? There is no other solution.

My number-one encouragement for people is to stay close to nature as much as they possibly can because without it we cannot survive. Nature helps us to take care of our minds, so it is important that we reciprocate and do whatever is in our power to help in return. Our environment gives us the air we breathe, the food we eat, shelter over our heads. When we immerse ourselves in nature in whatever way we can, then we make this connection in our minds and through our senses – we really begin to understand how interdependent everything is and how it is only through friendliness to both nature and each other that we can be happy.

If we don't each play our own little part by caring about each other and caring about nature (which does so much to look after us), how can we genuinely be happy? Each individual contribution adds to the collective effort; without one we can't have the other, which is why I so strongly believe that every single one of us can make a difference. Sometimes, therefore, we need to remind ourselves of the big picture, while at other times we need to remember to look inside and nurture our own wisdom and inner nature. It's all a question of balance and understanding the relationship between us as individuals and the world.

Pick up garbage along the way

It's interesting that Dr Mark Williams talks about people having a map, but not walking their journey (see p. 59) because, for me, the best way to bring clarity to the mind – to purify it of all the nonsense that naturally builds up over time – is to join the Pad Yatra that we do every year. This is because the Pad Yatra is undertaken with a beneficial motivation (usually there is an environmental significance – for example, we have walked for a month through the Himalayas picking up garbage and passing on the message to villagers that plastic does not degrade) and it also involves external, physical hardship. Embarking on these Pad Yatras, we leave behind any sense of modern convenience or luxury; some volunteers may even reach the point where they feel they cannot go on. But so often at that point I have seen a transformation: a person will finally give up worrying about how they are going to reach the top of the mountain and, instead, concentrate on each and every step. This is the point at which they notice the beauty of the mountains and the beauty of reason for being there. Carrie described this moment as pure happiness:

I will never forget going on the Pad Yatra in Ladakh. His Holiness and his nuns from the Himalayas were so fit and seemed to run up the steep mountainsides, while most of us 'foreigners' struggled every day to keep up. I couldn't stop complaining; it was freezing, the food was nothing I was used to and I felt terrible in the altitude. Every day I would just look at the top of the next mountain pass and want to cry. On quite a few occasions I did cry and I wondered why on earth I had thought to join this journey across one of the hardest terrains in the world. And then one day I thought I might have to give the whole thing up and ask to be escorted back. All I could do was focus on putting one foot in front of the other, step by step. Gradually, I got into a rhythm and my usual complaints and my aches and pains drifted aside in my mind as I took a step, and then another. I was completely and utterly in the present moment; there was no energy left for anything else. I know that I had to literally fall to my knees to reach this under-standing, but it was the biggest lesson of my life. I remember that day I had a broad grin across my face all day long. I stopped worrying about how far we had to walk that day and I started to truly look around me and take in the awesome beauty of the landscape, to understand more deeply why it is so important for us to do our best to take care of this world. I was frostbitten and exhausted, but I was happy.

I realise that not everyone can come on our Pad Yatras, but similar walking pilgrimages take place in different ways in other countries. Take, for example, the moonlit walk that women do together on a summer's night in London to raise money for breast cancer research – now that's a Pad Yatra! And there are organised beach and river clean-ups, where whole families go to spend a morning together while helping to keep their local environment beautiful and clean. So find your own Pad Yatra, if you can – it will be the best workout that you can give your mind.

TAKE HAPPINESS IN YOUR HANDS

There is a Buddhist phrase that means 'take in our hands', which is to take action or put into practice. So our thoughts and our actions must work together, like the wings of a bird – if we have one but not the other we will never be able to fly. It is not only our aspirations that feed our actions but our actions that feed our aspirations, they help each other. When you realise how united these things can be then I think this is a cause for great happiness.

I know that some people will feel they get caught up in the thinking part of the equation and struggle with the doing part, but as we develop our self-awareness we can recognise in our hearts when we are thinking too much and now need to take a deep breath and get on with things. When we need to say to ourselves, 'I'm going to do it' and take that first step.

If at times you feel stuck in anxiety because it

feels like you have so much to do you don't know where to start, I would encourage you to practise building your awareness of being in the moment. If you are feeling overwhelmed, then it will be very difficult to enjoy your tasks today, so give yourself a few minutes to calm your mind in whatever way helps you best. You might find that focusing on your breath is what you need (see p. 54) or you might prefer to go for a walk outside to feel the calming presence of nature.

We waste so much time, even when we think we don't have very much in the first place. I recently discovered that in many countries when a person dies the only thing on their headstone is their name, their date of birth and the day they died. And in between? Just a dash – their whole life summed up by a dash: '–'. It reminded me just how short life is and how important it is to be as awake as possible every day, and not concerned with being remembered – because when it comes to it, we are all a dash, really.

YOU HAVE SO MUCH TO OFFER

If you think you are too small to make a difference, try sleeping with a mosquito. HIS HOLINESS THE DALAI LAMA

If you feel that you don't have the time you would like to be able to give any attention to the world, or that you just need to get somewhere else in your life before you can really have a chance of being truly happy, I would encourage you to look at what you already have in your hands – you have everything you need. Happiness is the whole of life, not just what we think of as the good bits. We have to notice the mess and understand how it affects our lives. We have to educate ourselves about how important it is to alleviate suffering, rather than go about our lives ignoring it, pretending not to see it. If you don't know suffering, then you can't know happiness.

When we get back to the essence and really begin to value and respect our lives, then we will know how to use them in a fruitful way. The more we can free our minds from the constraints of labels and beliefs, fears, lack of confidence, inflated expectations – all the things that create a sense of clinging or feeling unsure about what to do or who to be – the more we truly understand what a gift it is to have this life and how we can get out there and make the most of it. We begin to know ourselves and our purpose; we feel comfortable and confident in our own skin. Right now you are in a very good position. This is your chance, now is the time.

WHAT WILL YOU DO TODAY TO MAKE THE WORLD A HAPPIER PLACE?

The man who overcomes his misdeeds with good actions brightens up the world like the moon appearing from behind the clouds. THE DHAMMAPADA

Let us use the present to live life happily and to the fullest. As I always say, happiness will only come fully when we share it, so we should always encourage each other to engage in positive deeds and keep our bodies, speech and minds in the present, living mindfully.

Great happiness can come from the smallest beginnings. We put so many things on hold in our lives – 'I'll start that project tomorrow'; 'I'm nearly ready, but not quite'; 'I've been meaning to get around to that' – and then whatever it is we are putting off gets bigger and bigger, all by itself it seems, so that making a start becomes harder or more complicated. But everything in life begins with a first step. Then you're on your way. What's the next step you can take, today?

Don't wait for others to love you. Why not extend your love first? Love with no conditions attached, with no expectation. Live the life you want to live, be true to yourself and your values. Always know what a kind and generous person you are. You don't need to take yourself too seriously. You don't need to be too attached to your emotions or your possessions. Wherever you go, your mind goes with you, so cultivate the treasure that is the mind. This is true wealth.

Be close to nature, take care of her and she will take care of you. Let your happiness shine through so that it may touch others. Is this not a wonderful life? We are all in the same boat, trying to get to the same place – let us help each other along the way and enjoy our journey together.

Everything you need to be happy is already in your hands. Take it easy. Be free. Feel the cooling balm of happiness and peace even when there is chaos around you.

Live with all your heart and be a warrior of joy and happiness.

When you realise how perfect everything is you will tilt your head back and laugh at the sky. BUDDHA

yellow
kite

books to help you live a good life

Join the conversation and tell
us how you live a #goodlife

🐦 @yellowkitebooks
📘 YellowKiteBooks
📌 Yellow Kite Books
📷 YellowKiteBooks